SHARING FAITH

This compilation copyright © Gavin Wakefield 2004
The author asserts the moral right
to be identified as the author of this work

Published by
The Bible Reading Fellowship
First Floor, Elsfield Hall
15–17 Elsfield Way, Oxford OX2 8FG
ISBN 1 84101 290 4

First published 2004
10 9 8 7 6 5 4 3 2 1 0
All rights reserved

Acknowledgments
Unless otherwise stated, scripture quotations are taken from The New Revised Standard
Version of the Bible, Anglicized Edition, copyright © 1989, 1995 by the Division of Christian
Education of the National Council of the Churches of Christ in the USA, and are used by
permission. All rights reserved.

Scripture quotations taken from the *Holy Bible, New International Version*, copyright © 1973,
1978, 1984 by International Bible Society, are used by permission of Hodder & Stoughton
Limited. All rights reserved. 'NIV' is a registered trademark of International Bible Society. UK
trademark number 1448790.

Scripture quotations taken from the Good News Bible published by The Bible
Societies/HarperCollins Publishers, are copyright © 1966, 1971, 1976, 1992 American
Bible Society.

Extracts from the Authorized Version of the Bible (The King James Bible), the rights in which
are vested in the Crown, are reproduced by permission of the Crown's patentee, Cambridge
University Press.

A catalogue record for this book is available from the British Library

Printed and bound in Great Britain by
Bookmarque, Croydon

SHARING FAITH

BIBLICAL REFLECTIONS FOR TODAY

EDITED BY Gavin Wakefield

ACKNOWLEDGMENTS

*I should like to thank my colleagues for their willingness
to offer their work for this joint project. In the midst of busy lives,
they have put up with my demands for their words, in the shared belief
that spreading the good news of Jesus Christ is at the centre of what we
are called to be and do. I particularly want to thank Steven Croft
for his encouragement in this project, and as my co-leader
in the module which first gave rise to these pieces.*

*Names in some of the anecdotes in this book have been changed
to protect anonymity.*

At the time of writing, all the contributors were tutors and lecturers of St John's College, Durham, involved in the training of lay and ordained ministers, mainly for the Church of England and the Methodist Church.

Alan Bartlett worked as a youth worker in Bermondsey before serving as a curate in Newcastle. He now teaches church history, spirituality and Anglicanism. *(Luke 7:1–10; Luke 7:36–50)*

Mark Bonnington teaches New Testament, with a special interest in 1 Corinthians and the book of Revelation. He is in the leadership team of a community church linked to the Ichthus Fellowship. *(Luke 4:16–30; 2 Corinthians 5:11–21)*

Richard Briggs teaches Old Testament, having previously taught New Testament at All Nations Christian College. He has written widely on the subject of biblical interpretation. *(Genesis 26; Ecclesiastes)*

Jocelyn Bryan is a psychologist with a desire to link that understanding with theology. She is the Foundation Training Tutor for the Wesley Study Centre and a Local Preacher in the Methodist Church. *(Mark 2:1–12; Romans 1:20)*

Mark Cartledge was Chaplain to the college, taught Practical Theology and oversaw the training of youth and community workers for churches. He is now lecturer in Christian Theology at the University of Wales, Lampeter. *(2 Corinthians 4:7–12)*

David Clough teaches ethics and doctrine and is a Local Preacher in the Methodist Church. *(Acts 8:26–40)*

Steven Croft was Warden of Cranmer Hall, and is now Archbishop's Missioner, taking forward the development of the 'mission-shaped church' report. He writes and teaches in the areas of leadership and evangelism, and initiated the Emmaus course. *(Psalm 51, Acts 16:11–40; 1 Corinthians 3:1–17)*

Robert Fyall taught Old Testament and is a Church of Scotland minister; he has written a number of commentaries, most recently on the book of Job. He is now Warden of Rutherford House, a research institute in Edinburgh. *(Jonah; Daniel 12:1–4)*

Judy Hirst teaches pastoral care and is a counsellor and a Church of England minister. *(Luke 10:38–42)*

Liz Hoare is a part-time tutor at Cranmer Hall and an ordained Anglican priest. *(John 4:1–42)*

Charles Read teaches worship and doctrine and is a Church of England minister; his lectures frequently include references to obscure 1960s British TV series! *(Isaiah 40:1–8; Isaiah 43:1–7; Jonah; Luke 4:42–44)*

Helen Thorpe is a tutor to both Methodist and Church of England students, and is a minister in an Anglican church in Sunderland. *(Acts 19:8–10)*

Geoffrey Stevenson is the Director of the Centre for Christian Communication at St John's College, and teaches communication skills, verbal and non-verbal (he has been a mime artist for many years). *(Genesis 12)*

Gavin Wakefield is Director of Mission and Pastoral Studies at St John's College, and has particular responsibilities for mission and evangelism training. He is a Church of England minister. *(Psalm 78; Philippians 2:1–11)*

Roger Walton is Director of the Wesley Study Centre, overseeing the training of the Methodist students. He teaches Christian education and practical theology. *(Matthew 9:36–11:1)*

David Wilkinson is Fellow in Christian Apologetics and Associate Director of the Centre for Christian Communication at St John's College. A Methodist minister, he is the author of a number of books on science and faith, and apologetics. *(Matthew 9:35–38; Acts 20:13–38)*

CONTENTS

SECTION THREE: THE EARLIEST CHURCHES IN EVANGELISM

Something good is happening to evangelism. On the one hand the use of the word is becoming more normal in non-evangelical circles. You can have incense and evangelism; and there is a book (written by a former member of St John's College, now a bishop) intriguingly entitled *Liberal Evangelism*. The idea that you could have a decade of Christian activity *without* evangelism is beginning to look extremely odd. Behind these various phenomena is the realization that Christianity always has been and always will be a missionary faith, with good news to spread and a longing for transformation of life.

At the same time, and on the other hand, some of the assumptions traditionally made by British evangelicals are changing under the impact of theological enquiry and argument. For example, the idea that there is one standard type of conversion experience— usually modelled on that of St Paul—is no longer presupposed; there can be a variety of journeys into faith. Nor is it assumed that conviction of sin must figure prominently in the preparation for conversion. Moreover, multiple conversions over a period of time are quite common, as is rededication and recommitment.

But perhaps the most far-reaching and, in my experience, controversial challenge is to the proposal that someone engaged in evangelism is bound to make a distinction between the saved and the lost, in order to target the latter. The main argument against this assumption is theological: who made us a judge and divider (see Luke 12:14)? Indeed, the disciples are emphatically told by Jesus not to judge (Luke 6:37). It is the Son of man who came to seek and to save the lost (Luke 19:10). There is a highly significant liberation in the thought that the Christian's witness is to all without exception, that evangelism—the spreading of good news—is not to be restricted to one supposed group rather than another, that the invitation to join the chorus of God's praise is made to everyone.

This changed conception of the purpose of evangelism decouples it from the idea of a one-for-all conversion. That is not to diminish the significance of conversion or, better, of conversions. But if we no longer assume that the task of the evangelist is to orchestrate for other people the equivalent of a Damascus Road experience, then we are thinking freshly indeed. The metaphor of the chorus of thanksgiving used by Paul in 2 Corinthians 4 has rich implications. Our task, we may say, is to encourage others to lend their distinctive voice to the song of creation offered in gratitude to God, Creator, Redeemer and Sanctifier. To do that we must sing well and attractively ourselves, and in the process make clear that there is plenty of room for another, preferably different, voice!

This exciting book looks freshly at passages from the Bible which deal directly or indirectly with evangelism. May it open us up to new and re-invigorated ways of thinking, being and doing in God's service.

Rt Revd Stephen Sykes
Principal of St John's College, Durham

HOW TO USE THIS BOOK

This book began as a series of Bible readings to groups of students in our college, as they were engaged in training in evangelizing and nurturing faith. We have kept them in biblical order, and I have written a short introduction to each section of the book, based on passages from the Old Testament, the Gospels, Acts and the Letters. Feel free to use the studies in any order you like! They were chosen by the speakers as passages which particularly encouraged them personally in evangelism; this is why there are some overlaps and, you might think, a few gaps. We are happy with that, believing that you too will have your own special passages of scripture which you might share with other people.

We have adapted the original talks so that they can be used by individual readers, house groups, or even a whole congregation wanting to focus on evangelism. Each one ends with a few questions to consider. Here are some suggestions for using the material:

INDIVIDUAL DAILY READINGS

Begin with the Bible passage. Take time to think about it for yourself, and then go on to read the comment and consider the questions. The passages are undated, but can be used one after another, to help you develop your understanding of evangelism.

STUDY GROUP/HOUSE FELLOWSHIP

Agree on a section for study, and read the Bible passage and the comment individually, before the group gathers. The material can then act as a launch pad for group discussion and action.

CONGREGATION

Groups within a congregation might look at different passages and contribute to a wider discussion about evangelism, as part of a strategy for encouraging the development of evangelism in a congregation.

HEALTH WARNING

You might like to think of this book as a menu from which you can choose items. Eventually, it will be good to work through the whole menu so that you can enjoy the full variety of dishes on offer. But watch that your diet is balanced!

It can become unbalanced by:

- Eating too much and taking too little exercise. All study and no action will leave you bloated and lethargic.
- Eating too little and doing too much. No feeding on God's word and too much action will leave you emaciated and run-down.
- Eating the bits you like and ignoring what's good for you! It is possible that we have done that here: ask yourself which parts of the Bible are not in our book, as they may be needed. Forgetting vital nutrients will affect your well-being.

INTRODUCTION: CHANGES IN
UNDERSTANDING EVANGELISM

This book focuses our attention on some of the varied motivations and models for evangelism, using the Bible as a starting-point. It is written with the assumption that evangelism is important, but that it may well look and be different to some of the older impressions we may carry in our minds.

Many of us cringe at the image of a man standing on a street corner with a placard proclaiming 'The End of the World is Nigh' but we are not sure what to do differently. We hope that the studies in this book will help you to look in a fresh way at what the Bible says about evangelism. To help with practical guidance on evangelism there are many other books available, for example, James Lawrence's excellent book *Lost for Words* (BRF, 1999), which has an approach to evangelism that is similar to ours.

WHY IS THERE A CHANGING UNDERSTANDING
OF EVANGELISM?

I suggest that there are a number of interconnected reasons for change, and I have picked out four which seem particularly important to me.

Firstly, church membership and church attendance declined in Britain across nearly all denominations during the 20th century. Virtually all sections of the Church are affected and see this as needing attention. Taking evangelism seriously is part of a response to a desperate situation for local churches in Britain. There are exceptions, of course: the new churches, previously known as house churches, have grown considerably, though some of those people came originally from other denominations. Both the black churches and the Orthodox Church have shown considerable growth, largely through immigration into Britain. In addition, some congregations in every denomination have shown numerical growth. Nevertheless, putting all that together with closures and decline elsewhere still means that overall fewer people attend church than previously; fewer baptisms are held, and even fewer church weddings take place. If we believe it is important to foster a more Christian society, then evangelism is a necessity, not an option.

Secondly, although the 'decade of evangelism' may not have brought in as many new people to churches as some would have hoped, the effort has not been wasted. In particular, experiments in new ways of sharing the faith and honest discussions about how to do it at every level of the Church and across denominations have given more Christians a positive appreciation of evangelism.

Thirdly, we are becoming much more prepared in this country to recognize that evangelism can lead to conversion. This might seem a strange comment, but awareness of more people belonging to other world faiths has helped to some extent in this area. For if a change of faith from, say, Christianity to Islam, is thinkable then change in the opposite direction can also be thinkable. Indeed, conversion from one faith to another is thought to be growing much more common in Britain. This does not just include the familiar world faiths but also other expressions of spirituality, such as paganism and Wicca. While Christians will have serious reservations about some of these other forms of faith, the more general movement by individuals between faiths does open up a space for sensitive evangelism.

Fourthly, there has been a growing recognition that conversion is usually a process that takes time, and so effective evangelism needs to take account of that. Courses such as Alpha and Emmaus work on the principle of a process taking place in people's lives as they consider the claims of Christ upon them. Of course, there are also important moments within the process, a challenging word from a friend, unexpected kindness breaking down an emotional barrier, an insight into faith when, say, the resurrection of Jesus suddenly makes sense. I like to describe what goes on as a 'punctuated process'. For some people, or at some times, the punctuation may be a comma indicating a relatively small change, and at others an exclamation mark for a dramatic change. There may be dashes where you pause, and question marks where you wrestle with difficult issues. The realization that conversion is usually some kind of process takes much of the anxiety out of evangelism and has helped to make the idea of 'process evangelism' more widely accepted.

WHAT DIFFERENCE DO THESE CHANGES MAKE?

In conclusion, I suggest that the new understanding of evangelism has these implications:

- When far fewer people have allegiance to the Church, the fellowship of Christ's people, we know that more evangelism is essential.
- When every section of the Church values evangelism, we can expect imaginative evangelism to emerge.
- When it is accepted that people may change faith, in any direction, we can expect converts to Christianity.
- When we recognize the punctuated process usually involved in conversion, we can be ourselves in evangelism and allow the Holy Spirit to work in people's lives.

We offer the Bible studies in this book as a contribution to this growing understanding of evangelism, in the hope that you will be inspired and better equipped to share your faith in Christ with the people you know.

+

Section One

EVANGELISM IN THE OLD TESTAMENT?

It is not immediately obvious that the Old Testament will help us with evangelism, with sharing the good news about Jesus Christ. However, these studies try to show us how we can make use of this part of the Bible. Even if the passages do not speak directly about Christ, they help us in a number of ways:

- Some passages help to put the story of God's plan of salvation into wider perspective: the call of Abram takes us back to the earliest days of God's covenant (Genesis 12), while the book of Jonah challenges us not to limit God's ways of working.
- In reading the Old Testament, we recognize that God's ways with us are consistent over time, so for example Psalm 51 remains relevant to our experience of forgiveness, and is a key element in the full presentation of the good news.
- Some passages remind us of human realities, which change less than we sometimes imagine: Psalm 78 is a call to share the message of God down the generations, an important aspect of our responsibility today. Ecclesiastes has a surprisingly post-modern ring to it and provides helpful insights into the nature of the faith we seek to share.
- Finally, there are those passages which are helpful in under-standing particular incidents in the New Testament. We have not made a point of including these but, for example, the study on

Jesus at the synagogue in Nazareth (Luke 4:16–30) refers back to Isaiah 61. The encounter between Philip and the Ethiopian eunuch (Acts 8:26–40) needs to be linked to Isaiah 53 for a full understanding.

We have provided a few examples: do consider what other passages might help you think through aspects of evangelism in the categories above, and indeed, any others which occur to you.

❖

GO FROM YOUR COUNTRY...
AND I WILL BLESS YOU

Genesis 12

COURAGE—PROMISE—FAILURE

Abram had been given a great promise, and it drew him on (v. 4).
We're not told he struggled or doubted, whether or not he debated
the matter with God for a few sleepless nights. On the contrary, he
seems to have gone willingly, though it was no small undertaking,
a hard journey for a large, extended family. He went with a promise
of fame, and on the way received the promise of land for his
descendants (v. 7). With high devotion, he built altars wherever he
settled, staking a divine claim for the land as he does so (v. 8).

Later, driven by famine to Egypt, it was a different story. More out
of concern for his own skin than that of his wife, he passes her off
as his sister (v. 13). This is a clever move that works at first—but
Pharaoh's morality is more robust than Abram's, and Pharaoh does
the right thing, returning her to her husband. Abram and his family
are sent away. He is shamed, but God's blessing continues.

Can these two stories teach us anything for our evangelism?

If we take this story of the beginning of Abram's journey as a type
or picture of our own journey as a Church towards the promised
land, perhaps they can. Of course, we do not have here blueprints
or strategies, techniques or methodologies for reaping a harvest or
proclaiming the word of God in the wilderness of the opening years
of the 21st century. Instead, we have a story that can inform and

enrich our understanding of the heart of God, and of the ways of humankind.

GODLY COURAGE

God's promises for Israel were not first heard among a settled people. The call to Abram was a calling out; it required a separation and a journey. We don't know whether he went with confidence or fear. If courage is not primarily a feeling, but shown in actions, then feelings of fear were largely irrelevant.

God called. Abram went.

It was never going to be a comfortable calling. As the letter to the Hebrews underlines: he stayed there 'as in a foreign land, living in tents' (Hebrews 11:9). Hardly the height of luxury—but necessary to endure for the sake of the promise. That is our position as a missionary Church: God calls; we may argue with him, and with each other; we may lose sleep as we toss and turn and weigh up the cost and anticipate the hardship; we may blanch and quake and quietly throw up in the corner—but eventually we make the arrangements, and we go. And our feelings will not be recorded when the story is told: 'God called. They went.'

GODLY PROMISE

Abram sets out for Canaan. And then the obstacles appear. He knew that was the place God was sending him. There was one little problem, however: the place was already inhabited. There were Canaanites in the land of Canaan (v. 6). At this point, God gives him the promise that his offspring will be given the land, so he does not turn around and go back. He goes on, settling, building altars, moving, settling and building altars again, acting in the light of the promise.

How many churches go forth with the gospel, with good news they know is really, really good... only to find that their neighbours appear to have no need? They are offering bread to people who are

22

apparently not hungry. This is an obstacle to sharing the good news, when no one wants to receive, when no one wants to hear. The promise—and it may be one we cannot easily see now—is that through Christ all nations will be blessed.

Abram's call is like our call to mission—'see how the fields are ripe for harvesting' (John 4:35). This is an image to inspire, excite and draw us forward. We don't look at the 'now', at the mean sufficiency to which we have perhaps become accustomed. We look forward to the *fulfilment* of the promises God has made, that the knowledge of the glory of God will one day cover the earth, as the waters cover the sea (Habakkuk 2:14), and we act and continue to act on the promise.

GODLY FAILURE

There came a time for Abram when hardship turned to danger. Whatever the promises received, common sense tells you to take practical steps to avoid impending disaster. Fleeing famine, Abram moves to Egypt (v. 10). Here, he realizes his wife's beauty will attract unwelcome attention. Intending to protect them both, trying to be clever, he virtually prostitutes her, and does quite well out of it. Now it is possible to read this account as implying that Abram's wife was in the event divinely protected from suffering the indignity of Pharaoh's close attention, but at any rate the truth soon comes out. Pharaoh demands of Abram—and you can hear the outrage in his voice: 'What is this you have done to me?' (v. 18). This is almost the same question God asked after Adam and Eve ate the forbidden fruit (Genesis 3:13), and after Cain killed his brother (Genesis 4:10).

Pharaoh washes his hands of the whole affair, and Abram is sent away in disgrace. We might be a little surprised: not only that he lets Abram live, but also that he sends him away with 'all that he had' (v. 20). As the next chapter soon tells us, Abram had become very wealthy (13:2). Not a bad result for what could have been a catastrophic misjudgment. God's redeeming grace was at work, and not only through the afflictions that warned Pharaoh that something

23

was not quite right about this new arrival in his harem; God worked through Pharaoh's morality to keep Abram from settling down in Egypt, as he might have done, with the Promised Land a distant, forgotten dream.

A WAY OF BLESSING, A WAY OF SHAME

Genesis 12 begins with a sending and ends with a sending. At the beginning, God calls Abram, and sends him from his country and kindred people. Although it is the way of blessing, it is necessary to depart, to separate, to journey, to endure the hardship of travel, and to struggle with the uncertainty of stepping into the unknown.

At the end of the chapter, Abram is being sent by Pharaoh out of Egypt, his wife by his side, his tail between his legs. It is a way of shame. But the blessing that God promised has already begun to come to pass, if only through God's protection from the dangers that threaten Abram from without and from within.

So...

- Believe that God wants to bless the unchurched people you know, and take courage.
- Act in the hope that the promise God gives will come to pass, and will give meaning to your words, to your witness, to your work of evangelism.
- Look for signs of God's grace working in all people, not just in Christians.
- Accept that God's blessing will be seen in spite of your weaknesses and even your failures.

QUESTIONS FOR REFLECTION AND DISCUSSION

1. Where in the life of your church might God be promising blessing if you step out into the unknown?
2. When you have stepped out, how do you cope with the dry, unfruitful desert places?
3. Is a Christian evangelist ever afraid?
4. How can our weakness, mistakes and failures be redeemed?

FOUR WELLS AND A FUNERAL

Genesis 26

THE STORY OF ISAAC

Sometimes evangelism seems a million miles away from the confusion and complexities of working out what God is first of all doing with us. At such times, a little bit of imaginative dwelling in the world of the Old Testament can be just the thing to remind us of a bigger perspective. The story of Isaac can be one such encouragement.

You are Isaac, and this is your bit of the book of Genesis (see 25:19). We are at the start of chapter 26 and there is a famine in the land (v. 1). We begin by counting your assets. How are we going to get through? You have:

• God's promise
• a beautiful wife
• your father's well

Which of these will make a difference? You might have good reasons to be struggling with this question. God's promise is all very well, except that you actually heard it just after it looked as if your father was going to kill you as a human sacrifice (22:15–18). Understandably, you may not wish to recall that day too often.

A beautiful wife could be a mixed blessing, too. Dad had trouble when he pretended that his wife was his sister and he ended up entangled in politics, plagues and prophecies (12:10–20), twice (20:1–18). The second time it happened was in Gerar, and it all remains awkwardly fresh in the memory, without ever quite being a favourite topic for family meal-time conversations.

At least Dad had wells. Compared to the other assets, this one seems to be a sure-fire earner, guaranteeing serious profits.

The story of Genesis 26 develops in several stages, the first of which is famine. The first asset ('I will give you this land!' 'What land...? This one with the famine?') is starting to look shaky. You head for Gerar (v. 1), and we have to ask whether this is a good idea. Gerar is on the way to Egypt, which is always a symbol in the Old Testament for the old ways of economic security and spiritual compromise. When you get there, God stops you, as if to say: 'Thus far but no further!'

If there is one thing you know how to do from family experience in Gerar it is passing your wife off as your sister, getting everyone into trouble into the bargain. Which you now proceed to do: two assets down and one to go.

Thirdly, though the locals may be upset because you are earning more than them, at least you have the wells. You have them, that is, until the locals fill them all up with earth (v. 15), and tell you, in a startling departure from normal ancient Near Eastern civility, to get lost (v. 16).

'All's well that ends well', anybody?

You have not done well in the asset stakes. In fact, it seems to be a classic case of 'three strikes and you're out': out, in this instance, to the valley of Gerar, expelled from the local town. Nevertheless, you are not totally out of it. Though you are about to find out that this is your only starring chapter in the whole mighty book of Genesis ('God of Abraham, Isaac and Jacob, indeed—and all I get is one chapter' you are muttering as you pitch tents in the valley), it is not over yet.

You dig deep (as it were) and discover a fourth asset: strength of character. It kicks in when the going gets tough, and it is now all you have to draw on when things look desperate. Newly encamped in the valley, you reopen the wells from your father's times and start searching for water.

There is a simple way that all the great stories of journeys and quests always go: first time unlucky; second time unlucky; third time lucky. Thus, the strong, handsome prince does not get the girl, nor does the wise and intelligent prince, but the lowly and unnoticed one turns out to have the required qualities. Even children know the score: not Father Bear, not Mother Bear, but Baby Bear. The pattern is almost written into the way we tell stories. It was even true back then: not Cain, nor yet Abel, but Seth. We should bear this in mind in reading what happens next.

The first well (v. 19) causes a dispute and you label it 'Dispute!' The second well (v. 21) causes opposition, and you label it 'Opposition!' You probably got this snappy habit from family tradition: when Mum laughed on being told she would have a son, your parents decided to call you 'Isaac', which means 'he laughs' (21:3). When it turns out to be third time lucky (v. 22), where the Lord gives you 'room' and... you name the place 'Room!', we seem to have reached the natural end of the story.

Then (v. 23) you do something amazing: you decide not to stay and celebrate the expected happy ending, but you head off somewhere else. In fact, you go off to worship, in Beersheba, so named because (21:31) father Abraham swore an oath after digging a well (*sheba* means 'swearing'; *beer* means 'well'), which represented the first foothold in the promised land.

This is a daring and ambitious move. You refuse to take the first good thing that comes along and say: 'That's it! God's blessing!' Rather, you first go out of your way to give thanks, and *then* receive God's promise *direct* as a result. Settling for the first sign of blessing, tempting though it is, may not often be the wisest thing to do.

The wells meant food, and food meant security, but we recall that that had not been the whole of your problem. There were still the unfriendly Philistines back in Gerar who had sent you off on this wild well chase in the first place. Now they are the ones coming over the hill (v. 26).

This is one more thing you do not need, fresh from building an altar at Beersheba (v. 25) where you celebrated God's goodness in wonderful ways, not least by digging another well (the unusual fourth one in the series of three, suggesting that you have gone above and beyond the call of duty). A closing scene of gratuitous violence may be on the cards. Four wells in hand: is it just the funeral to go?

In fact, in that way that Bible stories have of turning our expectations upside down, the enemies have come to say a most unlikely thing: 'We see plainly that the Lord has been with you' (v. 28). Now they are the ones thinking that it must be time for a treaty. Thus, we suddenly find ourselves eating and drinking, celebrating a new oath and, for the first time and at long last (v. 31), we have *peace*— a peace that is shattered only by the news of the servants running to say (v. 32): 'The fourth well: it has water!'

Genesis is full of stories like this. The 'hero' looks a lot like anyone who messes up, doubts, struggles to be a 'blessing' to anyone in particular (including his wife), but does not give up when everything goes wrong. Perhaps it suggests that there is plenty of room in God's world for that kind of 'hero', plenty of room for playing your part in God's plan when you least expect it. Fresh from your stunning performance as Isaac: do you want to apply?

P.S. THE FUNERAL: GENESIS 35:28–29

Despite the fact that Genesis 25:19 tells us that this is Isaac's bit of the book, chapter 26 is his only starring role: the story of the four wells. His sons, brother-in-law, nieces and grandchildren tend to take over the rest of 'Isaac's story', until these last two verses where, old and worn out, he dies. He has played his part: four wells and a funeral. That may seem an odd selection of events to be remembered for, but perhaps the ways in which God wants to use us in his ongoing work of blessing the nations may be every bit as unlikely as that. The book of Genesis seems to suggest that God delights in such unpredictability.

QUESTIONS FOR REFLECTION AND DISCUSSION

1. Can you think of examples from your own life where a simple daily act of routine work has unexpectedly turned out to be used by God for greater purposes?
2. Is there a tendency in our churches to have standards of 'success' and 'effectiveness' that squeeze out the odd and unforeseen ways in which God often seems to work in books like Genesis?
3. How can we build into our lives patterns of thanksgiving and worship which can lighten the burden of working under pressure?

⁜

BROKEN HEARTS: THE QUALIFICATION
FOR EVANGELISM

Psalm 51

What do you think is the principal quality you need to be an evangelist? Some might say a winning smile, a way with words, a facility for friendship, some kind of special training. All of these qualities may help. But the principal qualification for a Christian evangelist is a broken heart. It's impossible to proclaim the good news to others until we have received it ourselves. Receiving the gospel means being changed and transformed from within: coming to know the grace of God, the forgiveness of sins and the hope of resurrection.

For thousands of years, Psalm 51 has provided ways to put into words the times when men and women know that they are far from God and need grace and forgiveness. The words for the psalm are for the moments in the journey when we know that we can do nothing to help ourselves, restore ourselves, make ourselves clean or begin again. The psalmist simply throws himself on God's mercy. There is no alternative.

The heading of the psalm gives the prayer a setting in the life of David, when he has committed a terrible sin (2 Samuel 11). It helps us still to identify with moments in life when we know that we have made a terrible mistake, hurt those we love, damaged the lives of innocent people through our own actions. This heading (and others like it) may have been added to the psalm at a later date to link it closely with David's life and provide one possible interpretation of its original setting. The ending to the prayer, however, gives the psalm a different setting in the time of Israel's exile (vv. 18–19). The very city of Jerusalem has been destroyed. There is no temple and there can be no sacrifice for sin. Some commentators think that the final verses of the psalm are original. Others think that they were added during the exile. The psalmist offers the only sacrifice available: a broken spirit and a broken and contrite heart. The ending helps us to identify in our own lives those moments when all our resources have run out. There is nothing more we can offer. We stand before God in our brokenness and cry out for God's mercy: 'The sacrifice acceptable to God is a broken spirit; a broken and contrite heart, O God, you will not despise' (Psalm 51:17).

According to our modern idiom, there is only one way to break a heart. We see the heart as the place of romantic love. To have our hearts broken, therefore, means only one thing: that we have fallen in love with someone and that love is not returned. To understand Psalm 51 fully, we also need to understand that, in the Old Testament, the heart is more than the place of romantic love. My heart is the whole of the inner me, what's inside me: my personality, my emotions, my will, the core of who I am. It is this heart, this inner me, which is broken and crushed in the psalm through an awareness of my own sin. It is this heart which cries out to God to be washed, cleansed and renewed (vv. 2, 7, 10). You may want to explore other biblical passages which use language of the heart to speak of humility (Psalm 131); love for God (Deuteronomy 4:29; 6:5); wickedness (Genesis 6:5) and, most famously, renewal (in Ezekiel's prophecy that hearts of stone will be transformed to hearts of flesh again—Ezekiel 11:19; 18:31).

Although Psalm 51 is one of the most honest descriptions of human sinfulness, the psalm is also one of the most tender and faithful descriptions of God's love and mercy. The psalm is prayed in the remarkable confidence that God will forgive and renew. The words are for those who have come to the end of their own resources but find that God's mercy is everlasting. This remarkable experience of a broken heart, of cleansing and renewal, finds expression in a series of vows to proclaim the grace and tender love of God: 'Then I will teach transgressors your ways, and sinners will return to you' (v. 13); 'My tongue will sing aloud of your deliverance' (v. 14); 'O Lord, open my lips, and my mouth will declare your praise' (v. 15).

A broken heart leads to the experience of God's mercy. The experience of God's mercy in brokenness leads to a desire to share with others this cleansing, forgiveness and inner transformation. This personal experience of the grace of God is at the heart of what it means to share faith with others.

The pattern is there in many of the great call passages in the Bible. Isaiah's call especially echoes the language of Psalm 51: 'Woe is me! I am lost, for I am a man of unclean lips, and I live among a people of unclean lips; yet my eyes have seen the King, the Lord of hosts!' (Isaiah 6:5). Isaiah's lips are made clean, in his vision, by a seraph bringing a live coal from the altar. The seraph pronounces that the prophet is forgiven: 'Now that this has touched your lips, your guilt has departed and your sin is blotted out' (Isaiah 6:7). This experience of awareness of sin and forgiveness is followed immediately by Isaiah's call to go and speak God's message.

We find echoes of this connection between sin, forgiveness and a call to proclaim the good news in the Gospel account of the call of Peter (Luke 5:8) and, most of all, in the life of Paul. The testimony of 1 Timothy draws on the connections in Psalm 51 and Isaiah 6 in language which has meaning for those called to evangelism today:

The saying is sure and worthy of full acceptance, that Christ Jesus came into the world to save sinners—of whom I am the foremost. But for that very reason I received mercy, so that in me, as the foremost, Jesus Christ might display the utmost patience, making me an example to those who would come to believe in him for eternal life.
1 TIMOTHY 1:15–16

If we are seeking ways to renew our own passion for evangelism (or to rekindle the passion of others) then the way forward is unlikely to be in grand schemes, techniques or methods. The better way is to remember again our own need of forgiveness, the times when our heart is broken and our spirit crushed, and the unsearchable mercy and love of God for us in those times and in every other time. In our own testimony of the mercy and grace of God we find our calling to share that grace with others.

QUESTION FOR REFLECTION AND DISCUSSION

1. Tell the story of a time in your own life where you have been in the place described by Psalm 51. Is there a connection with your own call to share the good news?

❖

PASSING IT ON TO OUR CHILDREN

Psalm 78, especially vv. 1–8

I am a Christian because someone told me about Jesus, and some-one told them, and so on back and back and back, in a chain, or perhaps more accurately a web, of storytelling. It is long but not endless, for the links go back to the apostles and to Jesus himself.

A leading French sociologist, Daniele Hervieu-Leger, has recently written an important book called *Religion as a Chain of Memory*,[1] about the way in which religious tradition is passed on. In passing on the faith, children and young people are essential: have they picked up the faith or not? If they don't, the memory fades and will go. At the simplest pragmatic level, if we could stop the current loss of children and teenagers of Christian families from Anglican and Methodist churches in this country, then those churches would not be declining, and would in fact be growing.

In this context, a look at Psalm 78 is invaluable. It is mainly a recounting of Israel's history, but it begins with an encouragement to pass on the faith to the children: 'We will tell to the coming generation the glorious deeds of the Lord' (v. 4). This psalm provides us with a biblical motivation for passing on the news of our God to the next generation. It has been used in this way by the Old Testament scholar Walter Brueggemann in his book *Biblical Perspectives on Evangelism*.[2] In studying the mission of the Church in County Durham, I have also seen this psalm used in letters from a clergyman in Weardale, Durham, in the 19th century, commending the use of church schools. I am therefore conscious of being another link in the chain of memory by using this very psalm!

The special emphasis in the psalm is on telling the next generation the glorious deeds of the Lord (v. 4), the wonders he has done. The later verses of the psalm spell it out, as they tell the history of Israel, and they do so with an emphasis on the special and wonderful things God has done for his people: dividing the sea, sending out water from a rock and raining down manna from heaven among them.

This opening section of the first eight verses sets out five reasons for telling the next generation, mostly summarized in verses 7 and 8.

First, 'they should set their hope in God' (v. 7). The sense of the word 'hope' is of trust, reliance on God. By telling the story of the miracles which called Israel into being and which have sustained her, youngsters learn of their reliable God, a God who can bring transformation to lives.

With my own biological children, it has not necessarily been easy to talk openly about what God has done for me, though when I was a vicar they appreciated some of my sermons! However, it was a little easier to go to our church youth group and talk about why I was a Christian and how I believed God had been at work in my life. We can look for opportunities to speak in this way to those who 'come after' us, to encourage them to believe in a reliable God and to let them know that we really have met God and are not complete hypocrites!

The second reason 'to tell' is the negative version of the first: failure to tell, it implies, will lead to one of two false destinations. One is a wrongly placed trust in an idol or even one's self (see, for example, v. 58). The second false destination is despair (for example, v. 19), which is corrosive of trust in God. The hope lies in an affirmative answer to verse 19: God can and does provide a table in the wilderness! Here is one of his glorious deeds, which needs to be told, so that the younger generation will know that God is alive and active among his people.

To do this in our own day, it is worth providing opportunities for testimonies of God's faithfulness and challenge. I remember preaching about the importance of forgiving others one Sunday, and one man coming up to me afterwards and describing his time as a prisoner of war under the Japanese. The conversation was inconclusive, but a few weeks later he came up to me again and said that God had enabled him to forgive after some 50 years, and he wanted to speak about it publicly in a church service. It was most moving to hear him do so. In the language of this psalm, here was a man who had discovered further depths of the love of God and wanted to share his experience.

Third, 'and (do) not forget the works of God' (v. 7). We are to remember the works of God. If we forget the stories, our past, then we become open to other interpretations of events. A simple example might help: advertising often works on the basis that we forget what we were told about the appliance we bought last year. That computer was going to transform our lives; now it is virtually obsolete, and we need the latest model. More seriously, those people who claim that the Holocaust never happened in Nazi Germany are trying to tell a different story of the past, and trying to open up the possibility of a new interpretation of the present.

A church community remains a community precisely because it tells its story from one generation to the next. I don't just mean biological generations here, but also those who join the fellowship to know and join in the story of that fellowship. What has been important in God's dealings with you? How have you learnt to hear his voice? When have you failed to follow his way? Consider how you celebrate your own church's story, both for children and for new adult members. Without the storytelling, we would encounter collective amnesia; we would tend to think only of now, and only of us.

In his book *The Gulag Archipelago* the writer Alexander Solzhenitsyn tells of a Russian proverb that states: 'Dwell on the past and you'll lose an eye. Forget the past and you'll lose both eyes.' The proverb is a warning that if we forget where we come from, we lose perspective. At the same time, we are also warned about the opposite danger of only looking backwards, and so failing to see where we are going. In the context of the wider Church, we fail our children if we forget to tell them the works of God in our lives and in our communities.

Fourth, they are to 'keep his commandments' (v. 7), which makes a contrast with those who were 'not steadfast' (v. 8). I am reminded of the command of Jesus to love one another (John 15:12). As verse 8 of Psalm 78 makes clear, the people of Israel are not to be rebellious, but steadfast, faithful to God and one another. It is the quality of not being swayed by every latest problem or fashion (compare James 1:6). As well as a quality to be encouraged in the children of a church fellowship, it is one for every evangelist to take to heart: there will be times of discouragement and heartache, but just as God was faithful to his people long ago in the desert of Sinai, so he will be faithful to us in our own day and desert.

Finally, developing the previous point, the people are exhorted to ensure that their spirits are faithful to God. The last line of verse 8 puts this in the negative form. Right at their core, this generation is to be committed to the God who is upright and just.

Thus nurtured in the sense of the God who transforms people and events through his glorious deeds, the psalmist envisages a generation which will care for the world and for others under God.

Here, then, is a key element in the total task of evangelism: the passing on of good news to the young, not as brainwashing, but aware that we have a responsibility in the web of storytelling. This psalm encourages us to engage in the passing on of the good news. It gives us reasons to do so in the context of telling the story, and it makes clear that the active, transformative, wonder-working God is big enough to enable the next generation to live faithful, committed lives.

QUESTIONS FOR REFLECTION AND DISCUSSION

1. How is the chain of memory passed on in your community?
2. How can you encourage the passing on of faith to the next generation?

EVANGELISM FOR A

POSTMODERN WORLD?

Ecclesiastes

Back in the days of trying to translate Christian faith into terms that made sense to a 'modern' world, we learned all the reasons why Christianity was true: how it was simply more reasonable than any other approach to life, and how God trumped every other explanation for human existence. We were as wise as Solomon and as innocent as little children.

As time moved on, however, Solomon himself turned from displaying wisdom in pithy proverbs, and his wives wore on his nerves. He cast his gaze out of the palace one more time, watching people feeding the ducks, throwing their bread on the waters, and he changed his tune. 'Meaningless, meaningless,' he said, 'every-thing is meaningless'. The word was *hebel*, perhaps best translated as 'absurdity',[3] or 'breath', or 'mist'... gone like the morning dew. Life is pointless. You live well, you work hard, you judge wisely, and you die just as surely as the next man, who fiddled his temple tax returns and never weighed out an honest shekel in his life. This too is pointless, a chasing after the wind, or, as he might say today, the eternal wait for the next Internet page to load properly. Life seems to mock everything we can throw at it, so what is the point?

Then, while Solomon grew into a miserable old man, the modern world shifted strangely into postmodernism, and all the impressive reasons we had for why Christianity was more rational than any other worldview slowly turned into answers to questions that people were not asking any more. It's a funny old world: there are righteous people who perish and there are wicked people who prolong their life, and this too is utterly pointless (7:15).

Well, we simplify slightly. For one thing, Solomon probably did not write Ecclesiastes. For another, there was no moment when the modern world became postmodern. Rather, some aspects of contemporary life shifted out of one framework and into another. Despite these qualifications, however, the really striking thing is just how much overlap there appears to be between the cynical despair of Ecclesiastes and the bleak 'couldn't-care-less' apathy of today's postmodern culture. 'From dust we come; to dust we return; who knows what happens to the human spirit' (3:20–21, paraphrase). In fact, even if we did know, 'righteous people are treated like the wicked, and the wicked get treated as righteous', so why bother? Or rather, 'this too is absurd' (8:14, paraphrase).

For people trained in modern ways of thinking, one of the most frustrating things about evangelism in a postmodern culture is that a good argument seems to make little difference. For a start, what constitutes a good argument is one of the points at issue in the culture clash between the two perspectives. It is interesting to observe one of the key arguments of C.S. Lewis' wonderful book *The Screwtape Letters*: a good junior devil will persuade his Christian target that Christian faith is not based on absolute truth but is a matter of feeling. The unstated framework here is that such an admission would spell disaster for the Christian. Today, this kind of argumentative strategy is more likely to spell disaster for the trainee devil: what more could a postmodern person want than to find a religion personally and emotionally compelling, and what would be the point of considering whether it was true over and above that personal conviction?

Evidently, none of this means that postmodern culture is inherently better suited than modern culture to the Christian gospel; it does not share the same obstacles and barriers to faith, but it has different ones, to which the book of Ecclesiastes seems remarkably attuned. Life does not seem to reward righteousness, at least not consistently, and the wicked prosper. Generations come, generations go, and no matter how impressive your scholarship or spectacular your achievements, within a generation your work is out of print, fashions have changed—and you have lost your memory anyway. Meaningless.

Given that this is our shared reality, whether ancient, modern or postmodern, it seems that there were a variety of ways the Bible could have decided either to acknowledge it or deny it. Christian evangelism which tries to argue that the gospel is self-authenticating in its internal logic and supporting evidence fails to reckon with the presence in scripture of this extraordinary and liberating book of Ecclesiastes. As Christians, we live with a permanent inbuilt reminder that all the theological orthodoxy in the world will not save us from experiences of profound despair and jarring absurdity.

It is always tempting to try and 'explain' Ecclesiastes. Indeed, the ending of the book itself seems most likely to have been a later addition designed to round off a little downbeat philosophizing with a thought for the day: 'Remember your creator in the days of your youth' (12:1), as if to say that all that had gone before was what you get for forgetting your perspective. We should probably not move so fast, however. The words of the preacher which make up chapters 1—11 are not best served by being consigned to the 'wrong answer' box. The preacher does offer constructive thoughts in response to the absurdity of life: there is value in rest, peace, companionship, pleasure, justice, wisdom, and even in work (11:1–6).4 These are not knockdown arguments for the superiority of living a constructive life. The preacher is more than aware of the many and contradictory reasons to doubt that they all work to the good. They are, though, lived experiences which give value to human life in the face of absurdity.

It is this embodied realism that marks out the book of Ecclesiastes as a particular resource for commending the good news of the Christian gospel to a postmodern and blatantly unimpressed world. The book rings true. It breaks down barriers. It permits us a daring and honest self-evaluation. It even, perhaps, creates a space where unearned grace can almost seem to begin to make sense.

QUESTIONS FOR REFLECTION AND DISCUSSION

1. Is 'postmodern' a fairer label than 'modern' for some of the people you know? How would that affect what 'evangelism' might mean in your friendship?
2. How does Ecclesiastes challenge presentations of the gospel which seem to show Christians as people who are sure and certain of the good news?
3. Would Christians be better off pretending that the Bible does not contain a book that labels everything as meaningless?

❖

GOING HOME

Isaiah 40:1–8

THE STORY SO FAR...

God's people have been taken into exile, first in the northern kingdom of Assyria and later by the Babylonians and Medes when they defeated the Assyrians and became the dominant superpower, finishing the job the Assyrians started by conquering the southern kingdom of Judah. (The Assyrians had only conquered the northern kingdom of Israel.) So now God's people—the two kingdoms which split after King Solomon—are reunited in exile. They have lost their homeland and thus their identity. They feel abandoned by God—after all, hadn't he promised to protect them?

Into this situation comes the middle section of the book of Isaiah, thought by most scholars to have been written at the time of this exile (after 587BC) and so not by Isaiah the prophet of Jerusalem (who lived maybe 150 years earlier). If this view of how to divide up the book is correct, then Isaiah 40 is the first chapter of this new part of the book (or the sequel to Isaiah's original prophecies).

A RELATIONSHIP REAFFIRMED (V. 1)

The basis of the people's relationship with God was the covenant, and this was itself summed up in the 'covenant formula' spoken by God: 'I will be your God if you will be my people' (see 2 Samuel

7:24, for example). Here, God begins his message to the exiles by reassuring them that they are still his people and he is their God.

This is not a bad place for our witness to begin. There are plenty of people around who feel abandoned by God, and there are even people in churches who feel like that too. Often the Christian message has been caricatured as: 'You're a sinner and you're going to hell!' Not much good news there... Our gospel message would be more faithful to scripture (certainly to Isaiah 40) if it began with a strong affirmation of God's love for all people. (I know that the gospel does also call on people to repent and therefore makes demands for lifestyle changes, but that comes later in our message, not as the first thing we say.)

A LOVE THAT SUSTAINS (VV. 6–8)

Throughout this passage (and indeed the whole of Isaiah 40–55), we have a picture of God's love and power sustaining his people. Verses 6–8 picture God as outlasting the peoples of the world— perhaps the prophet is helping the exiles to get history in perspective. Empires come and go (the Assyrians went, the Babylonians have come and are about to go), but God surpasses them all.

Here is a God worth believing in! The world map may change; our office or factory may be bought out by a multinational corporation; we may experience upheavals in our personal lives (divorce, bereavement, mental illness—but God is still there; he still loves us and is still powerful. This is easy to write, read and even believe in our heads; it is much harder to live out. Years ago, as I went through a very difficult time at work, and more recently as I have coped with depression, I've been grateful for those who, like the author of Isaiah 40, have reminded me that God is like this.

THE DARK DAYS ARE OVER (V. 2)

The message with which this part of the book opens is one of comfort (v. 1) because the time of trial is finished. For the people of Israel, the exile is over. Shortly after this, they began to go home in groups. In this case, the difficult days of exile are seen as punishment for sin—although suffering is certainly not always due to that. Whenever we go through a hard time, whether it's our fault or not, we tend to think it will never end (and when things are going well, pessimistically we think it will not last!). The good news here is that it is over. God and Israel can get back together again in a renewed covenant relationship.

Paul Tillich was a very influential 20th-century theologian. His favourite way of describing sin was to talk about alienation. He thought this was the image of sin best understood by his contemporaries. We live in a world of broken relationships—people alienated from each other, nations alienated from nations. In Isaiah 40, the prophet uses the image of the penalty being paid and the term being completed. An important part of our evangelistic message is that the price has been paid, the time of alienation has ended and people can get back together with God. It is not just non-Christians who need to hear this: I find lots of Christians who need to be reminded of this. Too many Christians seem to think they have put themselves beyond God's reach. But whatever they have done, or whatever has been done to them, the time of trial has ended and there is the chance of a new start.

GOD IS BACK WHERE GOD BELONGS (VV. 3–5, 9)

The purpose of this return from exile is to glorify God (v. 5). Ultimately, this great rescue of the people is not for their benefit; it is to bring glory to God in a very visible way ('all people shall see it'). God is the centre of the message (v. 9). Nothing is to get in the way of this—hence the road-building project in verses 3–4. Hills are to be levelled and valleys filled in, all so that God can take his rightful place. Perhaps it is not too much to suggest that a besetting temptation in evangelism is to nudge God out of his rightful place and put our splendid evangelistic efforts there. If we keep God at the centre of our evangelism, then it won't ultimately matter if five people or fifty turn up to an event. What matters is that when people come to faith, God gets the credit, not us.

In exile, the Israelites were being told that their God was impotent: he had let them be captured, so he must be weaker than the Assyrian and Babylonian gods, mustn't he? Against this kind of pressure, Isaiah 40–55 tells the people that God still loves them and he is still powerful (vv. 10–11 combine these two messages neatly). Perhaps times haven't changed very much, because today we still need to counter society's assumptions that God is impotent, irrelevant or has abandoned us.

This passage ends up focusing our attention on God (he is to be praised), when it began by appearing to focus on the people (they're going home). Human beings mess things up—they are unreliable and finite, but God can be trusted totally, and he is always there for us (this is the point of vv. 6–9). Evangelism that focuses on the trustworthy God rather than our own angst-ridden plans is perhaps the 'more excellent way' (1 Corinthians 12:31). And it's more biblical.

QUESTIONS FOR REFLECTION AND DISCUSSION

1. When have you felt 'exiled'?
2. How can our evangelism run the risk of nudging God out of the way, and how can we avoid this?
3. 'The primary task of the Church is evangelism.' 'The primary task of the Church is worship.' Which is right?

KNOWN BY NAME

Isaiah 43:1–7

One of my favourite old TV series is *The Prisoner*, starring Patrick McGoohan. The central character is a secret agent who tries to resign, but who ends up being held prisoner in a strange village. Here, all the inhabitants are known by numbers (McGoohan—the prisoner—is Number Six). One of the famous quotes from the series is the prisoner's protest to the head of the village: 'I will not be punched, filed, briefed, debriefed... I am not a number; I am a free man.' Even at the end of the series, we are never told Number Six's name (which is one of the questions the series tries to examine, that of human identity).

Jurgen Moltmann, the famous German theologian, was taken prisoner by the allies during World War II and was imprisoned at Norton Camp in Nottinghamshire. Along with a few other prisoners, he was allowed to attend a Student Christian Movement conference at nearby Swanwick. Here, he was addressed by his name for the first time in years. In the German army, Moltmann had been a number, and then in the POW camp he was another number. On this Christian conference, he again had a name. This experience was a profound one for him, and he refers to it in his books and lectures.

GOD KNOWS US PERSONALLY (V. 1)

'I have called you by name, you are mine' says God in Isaiah 43:1. Chapter 42 sets out the greatness of God (in contrast to the people's sin) and, in similar literature of the time, you would expect the next section to be a judgment passage, where sentence is passed by this great God on his faithless people. However, you don't get the judgment passage; instead, there is chapter 43, with its message of love and reassurance.

God reminds the people that he has created them and formed them as a nation and, furthermore, has rescued (redeemed) them—not least by now bringing them back from exile. Once again, they are his people and he is their God (the covenant is renewed). The fact of God knowing us by name is important in evangelism because part of our message is that each person matters to God. We are not faceless clones, cogs in a machine or numbers on a payroll. God knows who we are. To know a person's name in Hebrew thought implied more than simply knowing information: it entailed also knowing something of who they really were—what made them tick. In a society where people can feel anonymous and forgotten, this is a vital piece of good news. Sometimes we ask people: 'Do you know the Lord?' (meaning: 'Are you a Christian?'), and while this reflects some biblical passages about salvation, perhaps equally important as us knowing the Lord is accepting that he knows us.

GOD VALUES US AS MUCH AS THE NATIONS (VV. 3–7)

The author of Isaiah 43 goes on to say that God regards the exiles as his children (v. 6) and he will bring them together again from the various places to which they have been exiled. In doing this, he is showing that they are as important to him as the superpowers of Egypt and Ethiopia (v. 3).

Israel's experience was that of being sandwiched between two powerful nations: Egypt in the south and Assyria (later Babylonia) in the north. She was a buffer state, and the history of Israel in the Old Testament is frequently dominated by alliances with one or other of these great and powerful nations and the consequences of those alliances. Nobody really cared for tiny Israel. But God did. God does not simply love and work with the powerful.

There are many communities in the world today which feel like Israel: small and powerless, overshadowed by richer and stronger neighbours. I have spent much of my ministry in inner-city areas, and in the last place where I was the vicar (a very deprived part of Salford, known as Broughton), people certainly felt that all attention focused on the 'great nation' of Manchester next door (though Salford Council did work hard to see we were not overshadowed by our neighbour). Will anyone listen to the voices of people in inner-city areas? When I first moved there, I found that many agencies (the police, the health service and so on) just ignored what local people were saying. Thankfully, things improved, largely due to the efforts of church people. As I was preparing this Bible study, I led a weekend of events to encourage the sharing of faith, in a remote part of Cumbria. The area around Lanercost and Gilsland had been devastated by foot and mouth disease the year before. The people there also felt marginalized and ignored. To them and to the people of Broughton, the prophet here says that they matter to God just as much as London or New York does. Isn't that an important part of our message?

I AM WITH YOU (V. 2)

Faced with going on a mission, it is not unusual to feel nervous. Actually, it is not unusual to feel petrified. And then there is the sense of inadequacy. Are we up to the task? Will we get all the preparation done? Will our reserves of strength and energy hold out? To the bruised and battered exiles, faced with going home and rebuilding their nation, the prophet relays God's message that God's strength is available. God will be with them (and us) when it feels as if we might drown in the tasks that face us: 'When you pass through the waters, I will be with you; and through the rivers, they shall not overwhelm you.' Of course, this is a reference back to the escape from Egypt centuries before. Faced with the Red Sea to cross, the Israelites found God got them through safely (Exodus 14). Sometimes people say: 'I'm going under!' when they can't cope with life any more. God will see us through, and there are few better times than a mission to see that happen. It's also part of our Christian discipleship and growth, learning to trust God especially when it seems we are up against it and there's no way out.

McGoohan's prisoner finally escapes, but even then we never learn his name. Much as I enjoy watching videos of that series, the message in Isaiah 43 is altogether better. We are known personally by God, and he is with us.

QUESTIONS FOR REFLECTION AND DISCUSSION

1. When have you felt marginalized, ignored or forgotten?
2. Which communities in your town or area are powerless and unknown?
3. How can Christians apply this passage to the situations you have listed above?
4. Why do you think God behaves as he does in this passage?

HOW DO WE GET GOING?

Jonah

An Indonesian businessman was converted, and immediately began sharing his faith with his colleagues. He decided to start brief lunchtime services, where he could talk to them more widely. After a few weeks he sought out an English missionary acquaintance and confessed that he felt his strategy was not working.

'I've been holding these services for a few weeks', he said, 'and only 30 or 40 people have come to faith.' The missionary gulped and replied that if that had happened in his country he would think that something like a revival had broken out.

This story does not mean that numbers are a test of 'success'. Getting going in mission is often paralysed, however, by a lack of expectation that God will work and also a fear of being rejected. The book of Jonah is a great help to us in thinking about how to begin evangelizing and in considering some of the hindrances and obstacles. This is a brilliantly told short story with shrewd characterization, many twists of plot and a delightful humour. We shall focus on God, Jonah and the various people encountered along the way.

GOD AND JONAH

The God of Jonah is not a tame God, but rather the Hound of Heaven[5] who will not give up until his purposes are fulfilled. Three things about this God are noteworthy. He is the Creator, and that means not only that he once made the universe but that he is continually involved in calling people and making himself known and that he will use his resources as Creator to ensure that his mission is carried out. He sends a wind (1:4); he provides a fish (1:17); he commands the fish (2:10); he provides a vine (4:6) and then a worm to destroy the vine (4:7). Mission is not something we initiate; we join in what God is already doing.

This God also calls people, and he calls them with urgency. Chapter 1:1–2 is not always well translated in our English versions. More starkly, what God says to Jonah is 'Up! Off to Nineveh!' The call to go is unmistakable and a command rather than an invitation.

God is also unpredictable, and Jonah is astonished at the destination: 'Go at once to Nineveh... and cry out against it' (1:2). No question of cosy chats in a non-threatening environment; this is a call to ride straight into gunfire. Yet God is in control: three times in three verses (1:1–3) he is called 'Lord', 'Yahweh', the name God revealed to Moses, because it indicates his unbreakable relationship with his people. He promises never to leave them, and to complete what he is doing for them.

Yet while mission is God's mission, sustained by him, carried forward and completed by him, he chooses people to be his messengers. We have seen that the call of God is not like being told we've won the lottery or a holiday for two in the Caribbean; it is more like being told to report to the boss at 2pm. Now God's choice appears to be less than inspired.

Jonah's first reaction is to run away, and he heads for 'Tarshish'. No one knows where Tarshish was. Indeed, it may not have been a place name at all, because the term can simply mean 'open sea'. Jonah is literally going nowhere; indeed, he gets rather more of the open sea and the sea monster than he had bargained for. Mission is not an option; it is a natural outflow of knowing God.

Jonah is not finished, and in chapter 3 he shows great courage as he confronts Nineveh with the claims of God. His preaching is a message of judgment but there is an inbuilt repentance clause (vv. 4–5). The response of the Ninevites is overwhelming (vv. 5–9).

Jonah does not rejoice in his success, however; he lapses into xenophobic parochialism and is furious that Nineveh is now going to be spared judgment (4:1). This book is a powerful reminder that God loves the world, and that he cares for those we regard as beyond the pale—he uses Jonah! Our own instability should not deter us from mission. In most of us lurks a Jonah, oscillating between cowardice and courage, obedience and panic, desire to obey God's call and flight back to our own comfort zone.

THE SAILORS AND THE NINEVITES

Having touched on God and Jonah, we now look at those who received the message. We have two groups: the sailors and the Ninevites. The striking thing is that the sailors who come across as decent and caring (1:13–14) needed to encounter God as much as the people of Nineveh did. In the story in chapter 1 we find that God is already at work in the sailors' hearts, and they come to a genuine faith (1:16). They meet God as Creator and Judge; they fear him, but also recognize and accept his grace.

The other group is the people of Nineveh. Two important issues emerge here. The first is that God is Lord of the nations (all the prophets speak of the universal claims of God). This is based on the claim made in 1:9 in psalter-like language: 'I worship the Lord, the God of heaven, who made the sea and the dry land.' The book shows how sea, wind, vines and worms all serve his sovereign purpose. This goes back to the promise to Abraham that all the families of the earth would be blessed (Genesis 12:3).

The other issue is that God's grace extends to everyone. Two later prophets—Nahum and Zephaniah—are to pronounce Nineveh's doom, but judgment here is preached to open the way to repentance and faith. The response in Nineveh is spectacular, and encourages large thoughts of God as the Creator who will one day make a new heaven and a new earth, and as the Saviour who will complete the transformation he has begun in people's lives.

So back to our question: how do we get going? The book of Jonah urges us to be open to God's gracious initiative. It reminds us that it is his mission; the resources are his and he is the Creator and Sovereign Lord. He will not fail.

It reminds us soberly of our own fickleness and tendency to run away. It also reminds us that there need be no hindrance to God's plan. Jonah's mission did not succeed because of his wit, imagination and commitment, but because after failure, he turned back to God in prayer and obedience.

It reminds us finally that the whole world is the mission field, here represented by the sailors and the Ninevites. A book which begins with the call of God to an individual ends with that same God concerned for a great city. Call and concern—these lie at the heart of mission.

QUESTIONS FOR REFLECTION AND DISCUSSION

1. How would you motivate people to *begin* evangelism?
2. What might be 'Nineveh' in your situation?

❖

HARD LESSONS ABOUT MISSION

Jonah

Whether you think the book of Jonah is a 'true' story or a story that tells us the truth, there is no denying that the author is a skilful storyteller. There's the dramatic flight from God in chapter 1, then the incident with the fish (enough to put you off fish and chips for life—well, maybe not the chips...). Finally, there's the bit about the plant at the end, with Jonah the moaner complaining that the bush which gave him some shade has suddenly got a nasty case of death. In all this, I think there are some hard lessons about mission.

OUR MESSAGE IS FOR EVERYBODY

Nineveh was a foreign nation as far as Jonah was concerned. Maybe one reason why he did not want to go there was that he did not want to preach to foreigners. (Once, when discussing where to go for a big family holiday, one of my relatives rejected France as a possibility 'because it's full of the French'—an accurate observation, but hardly very astute.) The point of Jonah going to Nineveh is that the message is for them too. The books of Jonah and Ruth can both be read as 'anti-racist' tales. They both show God at work with and through 'foreigners'. At the end of Jonah's story, God provides a plant to give him shade and, when the plant dies, Jonah complains. He has also just complained because God hasn't punished the Ninevites like he said he would—but then, they had repented, so they didn't need punishing any more. After Jonah has

55

complained about the plant, God reminds him that he loves the Ninevites, and that Jonah should be glad they are no longer going to be punished—after all, aren't they worth more than this (now rather wilted) plant which Jonah has become so fond of (4:9–11)?

The obvious question for us is: are there people with whom we'd really rather not share the good news ? Are there people we'd really rather not have joining our church? In my experience, preachers ask congregations these questions rather a lot, but I think that's no bad thing, as this is a situation we are all too prone to find ourselves in. Jonah overreacts (he says he may as well be dead in 4:8). For people who really have been in the depths of depression and have actually contemplated suicide, this looks ridiculous—Jonah has no right to be feeling like that. Similarly, if we feel: 'If they join my church, I'm leaving—it just wouldn't be the same!' then we are overreacting. 'Get a life and get some perspective', we might need to say to ourselves.

OUR MESSAGE INVOLVES A CALL TO REPENTANCE

Jonah's message does call for the people of Nineveh to repent. We must never leave out the fact that the gospel calls for changes. The New Testament word that we translate as 'repent' means 'turning around and going in the opposite direction'. The Hebrew words, as used in Jonah, imply something similar (see 3:8, where 'turn' is used as the translation).

One of my friends, with whom I used to run summer camps for Christian teenagers and their friends, has a favourite phrase which she used at the start of the camp. She would tell the young people that we had all come on the camp 'to do business with God'. There is serious stuff to be done as part of becoming a Christian. We must not leave the serious challenge out of evangelism.

THE MESSAGE INVOLVES FORGIVENESS

Just as there is a need for all to repent (no one is sinless—see Romans 3:23), so there is the chance for all to be forgiven. The Methodist Church sums up the gospel message in its 'Four Alls', and the first two are:

- All need to be saved.
- All can be saved.

This puts it very neatly (and, in case you're wondering, the other two are 'All can know they are saved' and 'All can be saved to the uttermost'.)

Once again, we are forced by the story to ask if we are as generous, gracious and forgiving as God. He forgives the Ninevites and welcomes them into his family. Jonah would have preferred that God hadn't done that. Jesus tell us in the Lord's prayer to forgive as we have been forgiven (Luke 11:4) and the early Church in Acts 10 came to see that membership of the Church was open to all—including the Gentiles. This is a biblical principle and not just a bright idea by the author of Jonah.

MISSION HAS AN EFFECT ON US

When we go on a mission, engage in evangelism or help to nurture people in faith, it isn't just a one-way process (we impart the gospel to 'them'); we are affected by the process too. Here are four ways in which I think evangelism and nurturing people may affect us:

1. Resentment—we don't want to do it. Jonah was told to get up (the Hebrew word in 1:2 is *qum*) and go (*lek*). He got up all right (1:3) but the passage says he ran away (*brch*)—that is, he went, but in the wrong direction! He is still resentful in chapter 4, as we saw above.

2. Avoidance—which is linked to the resentment. Jonah runs away. We have a thousand other things we'd rather be doing. As the faith-sharing weekends approach, students often find they have too many essays to write (and staff find they have a lot of marking that needs doing). Anything is better than doing evangelism.

3. Learning to trust God more—inside the fish (in chapter 2), Jonah learns to trust God and to obey him. As we actually obey God's call to share the good news, we often find the same.

4. Learning that God will give us another chance—in chapter 3, God calls Jonah again. Interestingly, almost exactly the same words are used as in the original call in chapter 1 (English translations tend to disguise this fact). So again, God says to Jonah *qum* and *lek* and this time he does (3:3 repeats these words). Even when we disobey and mess things up, God does not give up on us, but will still use us. That's perhaps the most encouraging thing about Jonah's story.

QUESTIONS FOR REFLECTION AND DISCUSSION

1. Share with your group your favourite ploys for avoiding doing evangelism.

2. How can the group help members to avoid using these ploys?

3. How can we speak about the need for repentance without coming across as moralizing, or 'holier than thou'?

4. What experience do you have of God trusting you again after you have let him down?

5. Who are the people you'd rather not have joining your church?

❖

HOW DO WE KEEP GOING?

Daniel 12:1–4

This reflection is based on the NIV translation of the passage.

In Edinburgh's New College, which houses the Divinity Faculty of
the university, there is a splendid theological library in the part of
the college buildings which was once a church. In the basement
there is a small chapel commemorating a minister who served there
in the 19th century. A wall plaque quotes Daniel 12:3 in the King
James Version: 'They that be wise shall shine as the brightness of the
firmament; and they that turn many to righteousness as the stars for
ever and ever.' Many times when I was a student there I found this
was a place to go and remember the true priorities of Christian
ministry: turning many to righteousness.

Mission and evangelizing are the inescapable responsibilities of
the church, yet it is easy to lose our nerve. The growing tide of
secularism, along with the apparently inexorable decline in the
churches, can cause a sense of panic or, if not, an apathy and
grim acceptance of further losses. How do we keep going? What
resources do we have for the task? By resources, I am not
particularly speaking of Alpha, Emmaus, Christianity Explored and
many other excellent courses. All these are worthwhile and all
have been used to lead people to Christ. My question is more
fundamental. How do we carry out our mission and sustain it in the
face of opposition, apathy and our own personal weaknesses? Here,
the book of Daniel, written to strengthen and quicken faith at a time
of uncertainty and danger, speaks powerfully into our situation and
tells us of two resources we have as we take the gospel into the
world.

SUPERNATURAL HELP

The first resource is supernatural help, and this is developed in the passage in a number of ways. We have the ministry of angels. Here, in this final apocalyptic vision, Michael the archangel protects the faithful on the Last Day as he has done in all the crises of history (v. 1). It has often been pointed out that God chose fallible humans rather than angels to tell the good news, but we must not forget the role they have in protecting us as we do so. In this book, the angel of the Lord has already protected Daniel's three friends in the blazing furnace (chapter 3) and Daniel himself in the lion's den (chapter 6).

But there is more: the work of the Spirit himself. This is shown pictorially in chapter 7, where 'the four winds of heaven' (7:2) churn up the great sea and the four beasts, representing human power, emerge. This is a clear echo of Genesis 1, where the Creator Spirit sweeps over the waters, and is a work of the Spirit preceding anything that human beings may do. Jesus speaks in John 16:8 of the Spirit convicting the world of sin, righteousness and judgment. This is why we never go into mission without God's Spirit being there before us and preparing the way.

This supernatural help is intimately linked to the importance of prayer. Daniel had already risked his life in chapter 6 because he refused to stop praying. Back in chapter 2, prayer is the means by which he receives wisdom from God to interpret Nebuchadnezzar's dream. Prayer does not create these unseen realities but it opens our eyes to perceive them.

THE CERTAINTY OF THE END

The second great incentive to keep going is that the end is certain. Here explicitly in verse 2—'Multitudes who sleep in the dust of the earth will awake'—is the conviction that there will be a resurrection. This has already been implied in chapter 7 where people from all nations worship the Son of man, whose kingdom never ends. It has been foreshadowed pictorially in chapter 6, where the stone is rolled from the pit and Daniel emerges unscathed.

The times will be tough. Here again (12:7) we have the mysterious phrase: 'a time, times and half a time'. This is the period of approximately three and a half years in the second century BC when the Syrian Emperor Antiochus Epiphanes held Jerusalem under a reign of terror and desecrated the temple. In Revelation, this symbolizes the extensive but limited period between the comings of Christ, when mission is to be carried out. Nothing can prevent the kingdom of God finally being established.

Unlike Daniel, we live after the cross and resurrection, and we know that because Christ is risen there is an irresistible movement towards the new heaven and the new earth, and thus the success of mission is ensured. Earlier in Daniel 'all the peoples, nations and men of every language' had been ordered to worship the golden image (3:7), but in chapter 7 all peoples worship the Son of man (echoed in the vision of heaven in Revelation 7).

This is the last word in mission. At the moment in the West we face what seems like terminal decline, and phrases such as 'the tide going out' seem to sum up the state of the church, but this is not the last word.

All this may seem rather remote from the realities of evangelism. What about the difficult youngsters, the entrenched conservatism of those whose interest in evangelism is non-existent, the millions who do not find church relevant and the sneering contempt of the liberal humanist movement? All these are real enough, and a reminder to avoid complacency.

The real thrust of the Daniel passage is to encourage us to keep going because the final result will be wonderful beyond our imagination. In verse 13, Daniel is told: 'Go your way till the end.' The fact that the outcome is not in doubt is not an encouragement to complacency but rather an impetus to keep going and keep sharing our faith until the end of ministry and of life. Beyond that is the End when all the evangelistic endeavour is caught up by grace to become part of the experience of the new heaven and the new earth.

QUESTIONS FOR REFLECTION AND DISCUSSION

1. What factors are particularly difficult in sustaining evangelism?
2. In what ways does a firm conviction of the End help us in the day-to-day business of sharing the good news?

+

Section Two

GOSPEL EVANGELISM

We may often hear talk of 'preaching the gospel' or 'getting the gospel message across', but we may not always be clear about what is meant by this. On the whole, it tends to refer to the pattern of Jesus' life, death and resurrection, and the need for us to respond to God's invitation through repentance and faith. The reflections that follow on the Gospels do not deny any of that, but they want to stretch us in our faith and response to God.

This means that we have not always chosen the 'obvious' passages (how could we miss out Matthew 28:16–20, for example?), but we also want to look again at some familiar stories from a fresh angle. So we consider the importance of Jesus being on the move (Luke 4:42–44), and take a look at the story of Jesus and the Samaritan woman at the well (John 4) through the lens of spiritual direction.

Where is faith to be found? Thinking about Jesus and the Roman centurion gives some different answers (Luke 7:1–10). We can find confidence to speak of our faith in a sideways look at the story of Mary and Martha meeting Jesus (Luke 10:38–42).

As you read these and other Gospel passages not included in our selection, ask God to give you fresh insight into what have so often become over-familiar stories. Jesus makes a huge impact on people for the first time, surprising them, turning their world upside down: allow these reflections to upset your view of Jesus in some way and then ask for courage to share the good news!

✜

COLLECTING THE FRUIT

Matthew 9:35–38

I remember crying on the first night of the first mission I ever took part in. It was not because of the emotion of an intense move of the Holy Spirit, or because I was overcome with fear. It was because I was so depressed. We were a group of young students in a little Methodist church for a week. We had planned meticulously and prayed fervently, or at least we had thought we had. Our first night was an open evening for the church to meet the team, and it was soon clear that not many people in this particular place actually wanted to meet the team! Three members of the five-strong organizing committee had turned up (two had important commitments at the bowling club) and the only other person had mistaken the evening for Scottish dancing. It was not the best experience in sharing the good news of Jesus that I have ever had.

There have been lots of good times, but there have also been a lot of tough times. Missions that go wrong, churches stubbornly refusing to change, missed opportunities when fear rather than love has got the better of me, and all of this in a culture that seems so closed to the Christian gospel.

One of the ways I am sustained in tough times is through this passage from Matthew. Jesus teaches his young students before sending them out on their first mission. It forms a link between the teaching and actions of Jesus and what he expects of his disciples.

What does he want them to see?

AMAZING POSSIBILITIES

For Jesus, the harvest is 'plentiful' (v. 37). When we look at our own situation, would we say that the harvest is plentiful? We may struggle in our own churches to get people to make the after-service coffee rather than have people queuing for hours to get into the church. Too often the world seems to be more interested in getting drunk on a Saturday evening than coming to church on a Sunday morning.

Matthew gives us a couple of clues as to why Jesus saw such amazing possibilities for his inexperienced followers. First, Jesus *met* people where they really were. In verse 35, we learn that he went out to all of the towns and villages teaching, preaching and healing. He took the initiative and got involved.

What does that mean for the way we talk about priorities in church? Is the bowling club in fact more important than the church committee? Are we meeting people on their terms, or do we subconsciously want people to come to us before we are prepared to tell them about Jesus? The God of the Christian faith did not wait for us to come to him but while we were still sinners he came into our world in Jesus and died our death on the cross (Romans 5:8). His disciples are called to follow such a pattern.

Second, Jesus *saw* people as they really were. He not only met with them but he also saw their needs (v. 36). He saw people harassed, helpless, and as sheep without a shepherd, having no direction or purpose in life and not knowing the one who cares for them.

This was not a kind of arrogant judgmentalism looking down and condemning people. It stemmed from the deep compassion that Jesus had for the women and men, boys and girls he met. The word used for 'compassion' is the strongest word in the Greek language for pity. It means 'stomach-churning' compassion that sees the love of God and the desperate needs of those he loves. In sharing our faith, we need to listen with compassion and ask to see others as God sees them.

If we go to where people are and see people as they really are, then we too may begin to see the amazing possibilities of a plentiful harvest.

INCREDIBLE PROBLEM

If Jesus is encouraging a big vision for his disciples, he is also a realist. The harvest might be plentiful but the workers are few (v. 37). The story is told of a strike at a Bombay cemetery. On the day of the strike, the manager had put up a sign that said: 'This morning there will only be a skeleton staff'!

We might as well put up such a sign outside many of our churches. Evangelism is one of those words that makes many Christians run, not in the direction of Nineveh but in completely the opposite direction of Tarshish. At the same time, it is very easy to condemn others in church with: 'If only they were really on fire in their faith they would be bringing people to church.'

Such criticism misses the point. Jesus is not condemning the crowd. He is just being real with the disciples. He is saying: 'This is the way that it is. It is going to be a tough job, so don't direct your energy into criticizing others, but get on with the task to which I have called you.'

Most church leaders should know that you cannot get people involved in ongoing evangelism and personal witness by making them feel bad about themselves. People get involved in evangelism by being given confidence. We need a few good role models; we need to see it work and we need gentle encouragement.

The disciples could complain about the incredible problem of so few workers, or they could get on and provide the models for others to follow.

EXTRAORDINARY POWER

In all of the difficulties of evangelism, there is one factor that can easily be ignored: the Lord of the harvest provides the power for the harvest to be brought in. Jesus says, 'Ask the Lord of the harvest to send out labourers into his harvest' (v. 38). It is a reminder of our dependency on and partnership with the Lord himself in all of this.

A school was closed one day because of snow. On her return to school the next day, a girl was asked whether she had used the time effectively. 'Yes,' she said, 'I prayed for more snow!' Do we as individuals or as churches see prayer as an effective use of time? If we did, would we spend more time doing it?

Prayer is the simple recognition that we need the power of the Spirit to help us to witness, for mission is the work of the Spirit in us and through us. The Spirit alone helps us to bear witness, casts out fear, transforms our character, enables our church to be the body of Christ, and gives us the compassion to love the lost.

Prayer and action go together. Jesus tells the disciples to pray for workers and then they become the answer to their own prayer (10:5)! Sometimes you need to be ready for that!

The theologian A.M. Hunter once said that the gospel is about 'unremarkable beginnings, unimaginable endings'. The disciples who heard these words of Jesus would see that in their lives. Let us ask the Lord of the harvest that we would have the same experience.

And by the way, I was also crying at the end of my first student mission—but for a very different reason!

QUESTIONS FOR REFLECTION AND DISCUSSION

1. How many of our friends are not Christians? How do we develop such friendships?
2. How have we been encouraged in trying to share our faith?

LOVE: THE INSPIRATION, AUTHORITY AND SUSTAINING ENERGY OF EVANGELISM

Matthew 9:36—11:1

There are several accounts of Jesus sending out his disciples on a mission (Mark 6:7–13; Matthew 10:1–42; Luke 9:1–11; 10:1–20). All three synoptic Gospels carry at least one account; Luke has two. This may represent the fact that there were several occasions when disciples were sent on a mission during the ministry of Jesus. Alternatively, even if there was in fact only one or perhaps two occasions, it suggests that each writer feels a need to record a version of the sending as something that is close to the heart of the gospel and the calling of the Church. For those engaged in evangelism, they are key texts.

I want to concentrate on the mission recorded in Matthew 9 and 10, for the particular insights that this passage brings. I do this for two reasons. First, Matthew's version is the longest of all the four accounts. He has clearly taken texts from a variety of places and added other details for some purpose. Second, in this extended version, Matthew incorporates some seemingly strange elements that need explanation.

Here are three ideas to ponder:

Matthew emphasizes the idea that mission begins in the compassion of God: The story of the mission does not begin in chapter 10 verse 1, where Jesus calls the disciples together to send them out, but in the previous chapter (9:36). It is when Jesus looks around at the crowd that he feels compassion for them because they are 'harassed and helpless' and 'like sheep without a shepherd', so he turns to his disciples and asks them to pray to God for labourers. The starting-point was the compassion which Jesus felt, reflecting for us the compassion of God.

That mission often begins in compassion is evident from history. When John Wesley first visited one of the pit villages of Newcastle in 1742 he records how he felt compassion for children and adults in their poverty and lostness. He then established one of the centres of his work in Newcastle and worked tirelessly preaching the gospel among the mine workers of the north-east. Likewise, Francis of Assisi was moved to embrace an evangelistic lifestyle by the compassion he felt for the poor. Those who do not feel some compassion for the pain and alienation of other human beings will not be true evangelists. But it is not simply a human compassion. The passage reminds us that this is God's mission and it arises out of God's compassion. It has been seen already in the call to Moses ('I have observed the misery of my people... I have heard their cry'—Exodus 3:7), and rehearsed in the prophet Hosea. Paul points it out dramatically in the book of Romans—when we were 'weak', 'sinners' and 'enemies', God proved his love for us (Romans 5:6–11). The mission we share is God's mission, which arises out of God's compassion for the world. When we lose sight of God's love for people and do not experience and express it ourselves, we have little to offer others.

Matthew calls those who participate in mission 'apostles': Here (10:1–8), Jesus calls to himself the Twelve and gives them a new title. They are no longer simply disciples—'learners'; rather, they are 'apostles'—ones who are sent. This is the first time Matthew has used this word. Although his readers would know that these named people were the first apostles, Matthew implies it was at this point that they received the title. Mark and Luke both name the Twelve as apostles much earlier in their Gospel story. Matthew, however, is careful not to use the term until now. He wants to make the purpose of the calling clear. They are called and appointed in order to be sent: to preach, to heal the sick, to cast out demons, to cleanse lepers, to raise the dead. All the things that Jesus has been doing, they are sent to do. They are no longer passengers with Jesus as the driver; they are workers sent out into the fields to share in the harvesting.

With that sending comes the finding of their identity and authority. Its apostolic nature is one of the four marks of the Church (One, Holy, Catholic and Apostolic). Like these individuals who are named at the point at which they participate in mission, the Church gains its identity and authority in its 'sent-ness', its participation in God's mission. To ensure that this authority is not misunderstood, Matthew reminds the newly commissioned apostles that they are being sent out 'like sheep into the midst of wolves' (10:16). In other words, apostles carry their authority through vulnerability, always open to the possibility of rejection, pain and even death. For the authority of God is the exposed love with which he comes to challenge and transform. This love is both powerful (it commands demons and cures the sick) and vulnerable (it can be crucified). They need to be 'wise as serpents and innocent as doves' (10:16) for they move in a new world where love is the only base for authorization and direction. To participate in evangelism is to find a new identity and authority in the vulnerable love of God.

Matthew records that the mission is to the Jews: 'Go nowhere among the Gentiles, and enter no town of the Samaritans, but go rather to the lost sheep of the house of Israel' (10:5–6). Matthew is the only one of the evangelists who makes the mission so focused and exclusive. This is surprising, as by the time Matthew is writing the Christian community is made of both Jews and Gentiles. While his may be a largely Jewish Christian church, he is painfully aware of the separation from other Jews. Why does he retain the exclusive command, when it would quite easy to drop this verse from the narrative without doing any damage to the general flow of the text? It may be a desire to be a faithful historian and record what Jesus said at the time, though the changing around of sources in this passage is against this view. Rather, it would suggest that this church community had an ongoing mission to Jewish people, despite their apparent rejection of Jesus.

One of the problems facing many Christians seeking to share the good news in Britain, and in other parts of the Western world, is that it has been evangelized before and, compared to some regions where the gospel is heard with readiness and enthusiasm, people appear to have developed immunity or cynicism, or have become apathetic or even resistant to the gospel. The continuing commitment to share good news with those who are increasingly hostile, as verse 17 onwards suggests, is for Matthew another strong signal of the love of God at the heart of this enterprise. 'Love never gives up' is the Good News Bible's translation of 1 Corinthians 13:7 and a reminder to us that even when there is little evidence of desire and even resistance we may be (particularly) called to mission.

Evangelism according to Matthew, then, is rooted in love. It begins in the compassion of God, finds identity and authority in vulnerable love and, even where it is difficult, it does not give up, just like the love of God.

QUESTIONS FOR REFLECTION AND DISCUSSION

1. Work through all four passages (Mark 6:7–13; Matthew 10:1–42; Luke 9:1–11; 10:1–20). Try to describe the main emphasis of each in a sentence and then compare the passages with each other. What does each have to say about evangelism?
2. Is compassion essential to evangelism, or should we do it because we are commanded to do so (Matthew 28:16–20), whether we feel compassion or not?
3. What is the hardest place of evangelism for you? Family, home church, a different or similar social or cultural group from your own? Why do you think this is the most difficult place?

✢

THE HEALING OF THE PARALYSED MAN

Mark 2:1–12

This is a very dramatic healing story. Crowds had gathered in Capernaum at the house where Jesus was. The place was heaving. Outside the main door, there was probably pushing and shoving, as people strained to get close to Jesus and listen to what he was saying. Four men came to the house carrying their friend, paralysed, on a pallet. For whatever reason, they believed that Jesus could heal him. These were determined men, desperate not to miss this opportunity for their friend. Realizing that they could not get close to Jesus because of the crowd, they carried their friend up the outside stairs of the house and dug (I assume with their bare hands) a hole big enough to lower him on the pallet down to Jesus. When Jesus realized their faith he said to the paralysed man: 'Son, your sins are forgiven' (v. 5).

There are of course many elements to this story, but the question I want to consider is: what was it about Jesus that gave these men their faith? Why did they see him as special, having healing powers? I hope that by reflecting on these questions we might gain some insight into some fundamentals of evangelism.

The Gospels present us with a record of how the disciples and many other people experienced a life-changing, personal encounter with Jesus. He had the power to transform people, physically, intellectually and spiritually. Through Jesus, people engaged with the great 'beyond', who is at the heart of all creation. This was and remains inexplicable, but this mysterious experience, this experience of something new and exciting, challenged what they knew and had been taught, and was something which they wanted more of. It touched a desire deep within them. It was powerful, so powerful that people left their jobs, relinquished their old traditions, took unthinkable risks and immersed themselves in the newness of life and hope which Jesus embodied. Who Jesus was and what he did empowered people, gave them courage to believe in a new understanding of the kingdom of God and embark on a new relationship with God. Through their encounter with Jesus, people were changed, and it was the courage, belief and witness of these people which was fundamental to the gospel message spreading out from Palestine to the rest of the world.

Each of us has key figures in our lives; these people influence us and shape who we are and who we are to become. When positive, these formative relationships are enriching, nurturing, even inspirational and life-changing. The teacher with enthusiasm for their subject and belief in a child's ability can have a profound influence on that child's life, giving them the desire to know more and taste the sheer excitement that knowledge can bring. This is a transformational encounter, a life-changing relationship.

In many cases, this change is brought about through trust or confidence: the confidence of the one who is influential and also the other person's trust or belief in the authority of that particular individual. Jesus was clearly a man who inspired confidence; people were willing to entrust everything—even, in many cases, their whole lives to him. He also inspired people to believe and trust in themselves, and love themselves. This was the significant point of transformation. So when Jesus said to the paralysed man: 'Son, your sins are forgiven' (v. 5) and, later in the passage: 'I say to you, stand up, take your mat and go to your home' (v. 11), the paralysed man and his friends believed he could walk, demonstrating both their belief in Jesus' authority and their confidence in themselves.

We read frequently in the Gospels how Jesus impressed the crowds with his authority. It seems that his authority was an integral part of his ability to transform the people who met with him.

Authority in Jesus' case was rooted in a lack of conflict between what he said and did and what he believed and felt. If there is a conflict between any of these parts of us, then we carry self-doubts, our whole integrity is challenged and we struggle with loving our selves. Jesus is completely dependent on God's love, and remains totally obedient to God, but at the same time he has a sense of his own powers and the authority given to him by his Father. This harmony between his belief in the love of his Father and his ministry was the source of his self-love and, in turn, his ability to love others. It enabled him to captivate people with his authority so that his teaching, his very presence, challenged who they were and the way that they lived their lives, not in a negative, critical way, but in a life-giving, exciting, hopeful way. Jack Dominion explores these ideas in his book *One Like Us* (DLT, 1998).

As Christians, we are commanded to love our neighbours as ourselves and love God (Luke 10:27, 28). This commandment was embodied in Jesus. This is what drew others to him; it was this that gave him authority, and it was this love that was the energy for transformation. If others are to know Christ through us, then the challenge for our evangelism continues to be our striving to obey the commandments Jesus gave us. How we minister to others depends on how we feel about ourselves. When we offer love, we are offering something positive, affirming and potentially creative. Our love depends on our confidence in God and what Jesus has taught us, as well as our confidence in ourselves. The ministry of Jesus displayed this confidence. This was exactly what the friends and the paralysed man realized about Jesus. Here was someone in whom they could believe, someone with an authority which was without hypocrisy and someone who responded positively to them in love. This has an infectious nature. Why else did the crowds clamour to be in Jesus' presence? Our first encounter with the risen Christ and our continuing realization of his presence becomes the source of our belief in the love and grace which he freely gives to us. This is the transformational, infectious energy that we hope and pray continues to sustain us; it is also the loving energy that we are called to share with others, so that they too may encounter and come to know the risen Lord.

QUESTIONS FOR REFLECTION AND DISCUSSION

1. Who are the key people with whom you have had influential or transformational relationships? Try to identify what it was about the particular person which brought this about.
2. In what ways has your encounter with Jesus been transformational?
3. What are the blocks for you in loving yourself?

⊹

THE WHOLE GOSPEL

Luke 4:16–30

The popular movie *The Matrix* is the sci-fi tale of how earth has been lulled into a computer-generated dream world by despotic machinery. Keanu Reeves, who plays the hero Neo, has discovered that he is the Chosen One who will free humanity from its sleepwalking. In the sequel, *The Matrix Reloaded*, Neo returns, this time as a messiah in search of his mission. To put it in 'Matrix speak': how must the One fulfil his destiny? The whole film is an exploration of Neo's messianic task.

Luke 4 is also an exposition of a messianic mission—the mission of the true Messiah, Jesus of Nazareth. At his baptism, Jesus had been identified as the messianic king, anointed with the Holy Spirit (Luke 3:21–22). In what is sometimes called his Nazareth Manifesto, Jesus uses the prophecy of Isaiah 61 to tell us exactly what to expect of the mission of the one on whom the Spirit of the Lord has come.

It's a text which is easy to interpret in the light of our own prejudices. For those for whom the *word* is central, it's a text about Jesus' ministry of preaching and teaching: '…preach the good news' (4:18). For those for whom the social implications of the gospel are central it is about the *works* of Jesus: '…setting at liberty the oppressed'. And for those charismatically inclined, it is Jesus' *wonders* that are central: '…opening the eyes of the blind'. Actually, of course, it's about all three: word, works and wonders, and how they coalesce in the life and ministry of Jesus. The explanation of how this holistic vision of mission all fits together is in the narrative that follows—embodied in Jesus' own practice of mission. Below are five observations about how this text helps us to understand Jesus' mission in Luke.

Firstly, Jesus' reading from Isaiah 61 and bold claim to be the fulfilment of Isaiah's prophecy is programmatic in Luke's Gospel. Luke says carefully that the Spirit 'came upon' Jesus at his baptism (3:22). Now we are told the purpose for which the Spirit has come upon him: the Spirit of the Lord is upon the anointed prophet for a purpose—the evangelization of the poor. Twenty-three chapters later in Luke's two-volume history, the Spirit will come upon the Pentecost Church in Acts 2 for exactly the same purpose: the messianic community is to preach good news to the poor in the power of the Spirit. Luke 4 is rightly regarded as Jesus' 'manifesto' for his ministry and mission.

Secondly, this Nazareth manifesto highlights the relationship between the Spirit and mission. When the Spirit comes, one of his most important functions is to empower people for mission. Sure, he comes to deepen our fellowship, to distribute his gifts and to transform our lives into the likeness of Jesus. But when the Spirit comes upon Jesus, the first Christians and us too, he impels us outwards to tell others God's good news. Our missionary endeavour has always to be grounded in the anointing of the Spirit. We speak and act in complete and comprehensive dependence on the Spirit. Any other starting point is to do our own thing, not to do Jesus' thing.

Thirdly, mission in the power of the Spirit is evangelism—proclaiming good news. This good news is not simply glad tidings, some happy message of God being nice to us. It is to proclaim the *euangelion*—tidings of God's victory. The classic use of this idea in the Old Testament is also in Isaiah, where the prophet foresees the messenger on the mountains running to bring to Zion the news of God's victory and reign: 'How beautiful upon the mountains are the feet of the messenger who announces peace, who brings good news, who announces salvation' (Isaiah 52:7). This is the announcement of the day of liberation, the restoration of the fortunes and honour of God's people; it is the news of the coming of God. It is this coming and this reigning which we see embodied in the ministry of Jesus, and which ought to be embodied in us as his messengers.

Notice where Jesus finishes quoting Isaiah 61 in Luke 4:19. He finishes with proclaiming the year of the Lord's favour, and doesn't go on to mention the 'day of vengeance of our God' from Isaiah 61.2. Later in the Gospel, when John the Baptist, who was keen on a little more 'vengeance of our God' than he saw in Jesus' ministry, sent people to enquire whether Jesus really was the one he had expected. Jesus simply replies: 'Go and tell John what you have seen and heard: the blind receive their sight, the lame walk, the lepers are cleansed, the deaf hear, the dead are raised, the poor are evangelized' (Luke 7:22). The day will come for the vengeance of our God (see Acts 17:31), but now the task is the proclamation of a season of opportunity and the unalloyed good tidings of God's victorious work and offer of salvation in Jesus.

Fourthly, Jesus' ministry includes the message of bodily healing, mental health, and spiritual re-creation. Notice another detail: Jesus includes a line which is not included in all ancient versions of Isaiah 61: 'to proclaim... recovery of sight to the blind'. This can only refer to the healings that follow in Jesus' ministry. That ministry is not a programme of social reform but a process of holistic transformation: sins are forgiven, bodies healed, troubled spirits calmed, the poor are blessed and the maimed made whole and restored to the people of God. Such transformations are the embodiment of the release of captives and the setting free of the oppressed.

When Jesus commissions the Twelve for mission, he does so in exactly the same terms: in radical dependence on God, they are to have power over demons, cure diseases, proclaim the kingdom and heal (Luke 9:1–6; 10:1–24). To put it simply: the one who says, 'Your sins are forgiven' also says, 'Rise up and walk.' The result is not just bodily wholeness, as if Jesus were engaged in some thera-peutic programme to help out the National Health Service. Jesus is restoring people to a God who cares about the whole of their lives and who, by word, works and wonders, reintegrates them into the community of God's people.

Finally, notice the two contrasting reactions of Jesus' hearers. They were 'amazed at the gracious words' (4:22) and: 'When they heard this, all in the synagogue were filled with rage' (4:28). Recognition and resistance. The welcome or the door slammed in your face. Both are there in the Gospels—in the parable of the sower, in the instructions of Jesus' missionaries in Luke 9 and 10, in the contrast between the 'plentiful' harvest (10:2) and the crowd crying: 'Crucify' (23:21). This double reaction is systemic and inevitable: some respond, others resist; some believe, others mock. This insight and expectation is essential to our missionary practice. It will toughen us against thinking that rejection is defeat. It will make us sensitive to those many who will want to hear. And Jesus' own teaching offers us a practical insight into how to respond: focus your energies where they are most productive (Luke 9:4–5; 10:4–12). Work with the responsive; don't waste time on the rude. Proclaim the gospel in the power of the Spirit with word, works and wonders to all who will listen. For today is still the day of salvation. It is still the year of the Lord's favour.

QUESTIONS FOR REFLECTION AND DISCUSSION

1. How does a gospel of words, works and wonders describe the activities of your church community? Where is there progress to be made?
2. What responses to the gospel do we encounter in mission? How do they make us feel? How does Luke 4 help us to deal with these responses?

⁜

MOVING ON IN MISSION [6]

Luke 4:42–44

This reflection is based on the NIV translation.

There is a long stretch of the A1 north of Leeds which I find rather boring to drive up. There are no cafés to stop at, and the scenery doesn't change much. But in August 1999 as I drove up there, every mile was significant. We were leaving Manchester after 21 years and going to live in Durham. I was leaving parish ministry after eleven years to go and train other people to be ministers.

Have you ever been on a memorable journey? Perhaps you have been somewhere you have always wanted to visit, or perhaps the journey has been especially long and difficult. Perhaps, like for me, the journey marked a big change in how or where you lived.

In Luke's Gospel, the journeys that Jesus goes on are significant. Journeys are used to mark stages in the development of the plot and to point out important features of Jesus' ministry. Here in Luke 4, Jesus is leaving Nazareth, where he has been preaching and healing up to now. The crowd wants him to stay, but he says he *has to* move on—it's part of his mission.

JESUS IS FOR EVERYONE

In verse 43, Jesus says, 'I must preach the good news of the kingdom of God to the other towns also, because that is why I was sent.' This is not the only time he says this: in Luke 4:16–21 he applies Isaiah 61:1–2 to himself. Jesus is the one of whom the prophet spoke, who was sent to proclaim release, freedom and new vision. This message is not just for one small group of people—it's for a wide audience. This is a feature of the way Luke writes his Gospel—he is at pains to point out that Jesus is the Saviour of the world, not just of people who live in Galilee (and if you look at Mark 1:35–39, where Mark tells the same story as Luke 4:42–44, you will see that Luke has shortened Mark's version to highlight the fact that Jesus must go to other people too).

The crowd of people wanted him to stay (v. 42). Perhaps they were hoping to see another miracle, or hear some more interesting parables—at any rate, they are not keen to let him go. Our tendency, too, is often to keep Jesus to ourselves—but he's for everyone. No doubt you have sometimes been asked (by preachers) to think of groups of people who might not be made welcome in your church. It's a bit of a hackneyed question, but it's still useful. We all need to ask it of our churches from time to time.

I was once vicar of two inner-city churches. One had a fairly middle-class congregation, most of whom no longer lived in the area. A family from the estate near the church started coming to church. The parents (and their friend who came with them) were all recovering drug users. They stuck out like a row of sore thumbs in our well-dressed congregation, and I was worried they would not feel at home—but they were all welcomed in, and the congregation was superbly supportive when, tragically, the family's daughter was knocked over by a car and killed. I was so proud of our church for welcoming and caring for this family. At the other church, a group of young boys would often turn up on Sunday. Some of their behaviour drove us to desperation—and sometimes secret amusement. (They turned up for a shared lunch once with a crate of milk they'd stolen from outside the newsagents, as their contribution to what Christians in Lancashire call a 'Jacob's join'—where you each bring some food to share.)

Jesus is for everyone—even those with whom we would not often want to associate. This is one big reason why Christians can't avoid evangelism. It's part of who Jesus is—he's to be shared with everybody.

WHAT'S THE MESSAGE?

Jesus preaches 'the good news of the kingdom of God'. That's his message—the one he *has* to spread to the other cities.

'Good news' is, of course, what the word 'evangelism' means. We all know that, but it's one of those things that we need reminding of now and again. It's another old trick of preachers to say that, all too often, we present the gospel as bad news instead. That's another statement that's clichéd but true. I find that a lot of people—including the trainee ministers I teach—think that God doesn't like them. Somehow people have this idea of a God who spends all the time condemning people. Whatever happened to the God of love who gave himself for us on the cross? Evangelism and nurture involve telling people about the accepting God. That's good news.

Most people know that 'kingdom' means 'kingship'. The kingdom of God is wherever God's will is done—where he is accepted as king. In the Lord's Prayer, 'your kingdom come' equals 'your will be done'. The invitation to believe the good news means inviting people to accept the rule of Christ themselves. When we give up our lives like that we find real life. Serving God is true freedom.

WHERE TO GO?

Off he goes, then, to tell more people about the good news of the kingdom. But where exactly does Jesus go? There is a throwaway line at the end of the story about him going to the synagogues. Jesus goes where people are most likely to be ready to listen.

Perhaps it's a technique that we could adopt. Start where people are. Begin with the questions they are asking. In my last parish, that was about feeling safe in an area of the city with a high crime rate. How you move from that question to the good news is something I'll leave you to ponder yourself!

QUESTIONS FOR REFLECTION AND DISCUSSION

1. Which groups of people are you likely to find hard to welcome into your church?
2. What are the big questions about life that your friends are asking? How does the gospel address them?
3. If the gospel is partly about accepting God as your king, what difference does that make to your evangelism and your church's nurture course?

❖

FINDING FAITH 'OUT THERE'

Luke 7:1–10

Before becoming a vicar, I spent some time in the 1980s working as a youth worker in Bermondsey. It could be hard work. This was before Bermondsey was 'gentrified' and, as well as some of the usual issues when working with young people who have grown up in difficult circumstances, we had groups of young men sympathetic to the National Front and supporters of Millwall F.C. We also had some remarkable people on our staff, but the most surprising was Dave.

He was a quiet and unassuming man, slightly built with a goatee beard. He was also an ex-Royal Marine, green beret and all. He needed some of that steel because he was our detached youth worker, working on the streets with the young people, on their turf with their agendas, not in the relative security of our club buildings.

We were chatting one day about our work and he asked me: 'Do you find Christ out there?' It was the wrong question for me. I had spent five years at a charismatic Baptist church and three years at a very sound evangelical Anglican church, and I had never thought of 'finding Christ out there'. I always took Christ to other people, because 'they' didn't have him. I'm not sure I even really believed that Christ was out there working with people before I arrived. I am still puzzling about this question 20 years later.

The passage for today has helped me to think a little about this: Jesus meets a pagan centurion who had more faith than those supposedly within the people of God. There is a similar story to this in Matthew 8, and there are also echoes in the story of the healing of the nobleman's son in John 4:46–54. We will look at the particular emphasis that Luke gave the story.

To begin with, we need a little background. Luke places this miracle story as the first one after the 'Sermon on the Plain'. (Luke's equivalent to the Sermon on the Mount.) It happens in Capernaum, on the north-west shore of the Sea of Galilee, where Jesus often based himself. It was in the territory of Herod Antipas. This tells us something already. This man was probably not a Roman centurion, but a foreign mercenary soldier in Herod's army. Centurions were most like our sergeant majors, senior NCOs, men promoted from the ranks—hard men, physically tough, used to fighting.

But this man loves the Jews (v. 5). He is a God-fearer, like Cornelius in Acts 10. He has built them a synagogue (v. 5). In Luke's version, it is the local Jewish elders who come on his behalf first (v. 3). Even in their words there is a sense that such a man would normally be beyond the attention of a Jewish prophet. They appeal to Jesus (v. 4), saying: 'He is worthy of having you do this for him'. This centurion is an unusual man.

The centurion is unusual in other ways. Luke tells us that he cares for this slave (v. 2). The word used means 'valued highly, honoured, respected, precious'. It is a strong word. William Barclay tells us that it was legal in Roman society simply to throw away sick slaves. They were just property.[7] Doubtless, people varied in their behaviour, however, and this centurion clearly cares for this slave.

The centurion is also a humble man. Matthew has the centurion come directly to Jesus (Matthew 8:5). Luke has him sending two sets of intermediaries, rather than meet Jesus face to face: first the elders and then some friends (vv. 3, 6). Both Matthew and Luke then report the same words: 'I am not worthy to have you come under my roof' (Matthew 8:8; Luke 7:6). This comes from a tough Gentile soldier, used to being in command, who might have been expected to despise anything Jewish as stupid, narrow or barbaric. So he has a number of attractive qualities—generosity, love and humility—but what moves Jesus is his faith. The centurion has discerned the sort of authority that Jesus has: 'Go... come... do...'

and it happens. He knows that Jesus does not even have to come to his house for his slave to be healed.

Jesus is amazed. He turns to the Jewish crowd following and says: 'Not even in Israel have I found such faith' (v. 9). Jesus gives pre-eminence to this man's deep and perceptive faith, pre-eminence for one who despite his qualities was still essentially an 'unclean' Gentile. Real faith is to be found in unexpected people, a surprisingly common theme in the Bible (see the story of Rahab the prostitute in Joshua 2 or the Syro-Phoenician woman in Mark 7).

When I began ordained ministry I remember my vicar going on holiday for the first time. Before he left he asked me: 'Do you know what to do if you are called to the bedside of someone dying?' Well, I had half an idea and Michael referred me to some other helpful resources, and went off saying, 'Of course it won't happen in the next fortnight; it's very rare.' Three days later there was a tap at my door and two young women stood there and asked if I would go and see their father who was very ill. I promised to come later but in the afternoon they returned, more insistent, so I went to their house, clutching the book that Michael had recommended, expecting a quiet one-to-one chat. In fact, the whole family stood around the bed as John and I talked and prayed! He died that night. His was the first funeral I conducted 'solo'.

In the months that followed, his widow and daughters came to church regularly and were eventually confirmed. Secretly I was very proud of myself. 'What a good piece of pastoral work.' But it slowly dawned on me that this family had had a long history of faith, of being involved with different churches. When I had jumped to the conclusion that they weren't 'churchy' because they didn't currently come to *my* church, I had completely missed their own journey of faith. Again and again in funeral ministry I realized that just because someone is not 'churchy' at the moment does not mean that they don't have faith.

There is a lot of talk at the moment about how we live in a post-Christian country, full of mobile postmodern people two generations away from the Church. This is certainly true of some areas and it *may* be that this is how it will be increasingly in the future. But we can also recognize the value of 'working with the grain' in local communities, of taking 'folk religion' or 'diffusive Christianity' seriously and respectfully. In many parts of the country, this sense of being Christian, of being people of *faith*, is still very much alive. We despise it at our peril.

So, when we talk about 'doing some evangelism' or 'going out on mission', I wonder if we need to ask ourselves whether we are simply assuming that we are taking Christ out with us? Instead, we could go out *listening*, looking for faith, expecting to meet Christ 'out there'. There are many metaphors for conversion and one of them is of recognition: 'Here is someone of faith.' And 'our' job then is to be a bridge, to welcome people home. We want them to feel that being with God and his visible people is like being at home, where they have always really belonged.

P.S. I still don't think I've answered Dave's question!

QUESTIONS FOR REFLECTION AND DISCUSSION

1. What sort of person would you be most surprised to discover is a 'person of faith' (as unexpected as faith in a pagan mercenary NCO...)? Why?
2. What would be the signs that someone has faith (but has not yet found a home in the Church)?
3. What could the Church (including you) do to build bridges for people to 'come home'?

❖

WHO DECIDES WHO IS WELCOME
TO THE BODY OF CHRIST?

Luke 7:36–50

Why are Christians so 'respectable'? Why was Jesus loved by unrespectable people? This story may help us to think about this contrast.

First, some reflections on the text of the story. It is particularly complex. There are similar stories in Matthew 26:6–13, Mark 14:3–9 and John 12:1–8, but these three stories form part of the beginning of the Passion narrative. There, Jesus is anointed as preparation for his death and burial. Luke does not have this story at that point but includes it much earlier in his Gospel. At first sight, this looks like a Lucan rewriting of a traditional story, which Luke links to the parable of the two sinners. Alternatively, it is possible that Luke had this particular episode as a separate story from one of his own sources and does not want to confuse the reader by using a similar event twice.[8]

The verbal links indicate some connection between the written texts of the stories, but it is difficult to be clear about which is influencing which. Matthew (26:7), Mark (14:3) and Luke (v. 37) tell us that the jar is alabaster. Only Mark (14:3) and John (12:3) tell us that it is pure nard with which she anoints him. Only Luke (v. 38) and John (12:3) tell us that the woman anoints Jesus' feet and wipes them with her hair. Above all, we note that Luke has some distinctive features: only he tells us that the house is that of a Pharisee (v. 36); only he tells us that she is a notorious sinner

(v. 37); only he tells us that the woman washes Jesus' feet with her tears and kisses them (v. 38); only he stresses her love (v. 47) and Jesus' love and forgiveness (v. 48). This is a very distinctively Lucan story.

The commentators are fun to read on this story. Some go all round the houses to avoid the obvious sensuality, even the frank sexuality of this story. One goes so far as to suggest that the woman anoints Jesus' feet because they are the only part of him to be touched by fallen human beings! I am tempted to see such a commentator as a Pharisee of the Pharisees.

We are not told what sort of a 'sinner' this woman was. She is seemingly well-known in the city as a sinner (v. 37). The most likely guess is that she is a prostitute, a class of women who were visually and socially segregated.[9] It must have been something very embarrassing and disreputable to account for Simon's reaction of distaste (v. 39).

The point of the story as Luke tells it, reinforcing it with the parable, is to show the difference between a forgiven sinner and a self-righteous religious person, between someone who is responding with love to the love of God and someone who feels no need of such love. We will return to this, but first I want to highlight the sexuality and sensuality of the story. There has been some deeply offensive material written about Jesus' sexuality, as well as much foolish speculation, but I am reminded constantly of Dorothy L. Sayers' heartfelt tribute to Jesus, that here was a man who did not patronize women, or put them down, or keep them at arm's length, but treated them as friends and equals. Jesus was at ease with women, and they with him.

Let's look a little more closely at the story. Why does the woman weep? Is it simply sorrow for her sins, or is there already some sense of acceptance by Jesus? He could presumably have had her ushered away, as hers is a very public and raw display of emotion. But Jesus lets her stay. More than that, Jesus accuses Simon of profound discourtesy in not bringing him water to wash his feet, a basic breach of manners in a hot and dusty climate (v. 44). The woman, however, is weeping enough to wash Jesus' feet with her tears. And then she dries his feet with her hair. It is a very, very intimate scene, and William Barclay reminds us of the significance for a Jewish woman, even a fallen women, of letting her hair down in public.[10] Then she kisses Jesus' feet and anoints them with this very expensive perfume. John, in one of those intriguing and vivid little sensual comments that mark his Gospel, says that the perfume filled the house (12:3). Here we see human beings relating through touch, smell and look, as well as through words. Here we see deep emotions of love and tenderness between a man and a woman. But this is the Son of God being loved and touched.

Luke reminds us of the shock of this. Simon the Pharisee goes straight to the spiritual point. This is a dangerous woman, a sexual sinner. We have been reminded only recently, with the Taliban regime in Afghanistan, of the ferocity with which such women are punished. There is a particular 'threat' and a particular 'contamination' that comes from contact with a 'fallen woman'. Hence Simon's frank disgust and therefore his dismissal of Jesus. Anyone who lets *this* woman touch him is not of God (v. 39). It is an open and shut case. It is, of course, the opposite that is true. This woman really loves Jesus and through Jesus, his Father. And so she touches him. (Whatever our disagreements, how can the Church of England have allowed the language of 'taint' to be used of the ministry and physical presence and touch of women?)

This is not some sanitized sinner, such as we might find in one of those rather implausible Christian autobiographies. Her familiarity with men, with touching men, is embarrassingly evident. Goodness knows how much of her life she had sorted out. What was she going to do afterwards? We hope she had a new life, but none of this is worked through yet. This is a profound and yet impulsive welcoming of a dangerous sensual sinner back into the family of God, long before she is safe.

What do we do with this story? Here are a couple of final thoughts. I wonder if it makes us uncomfortable, really uncomfortable, even if we don't say so? This is the sort of unrespectable person who certainly wouldn't be found in our churches regularly. I wonder if we even meet such people very often? Most of my friends now seem to be clergy, which is a very sad state of affairs! How am I, in the midst of the frantic busyness of the modern church, to find time to go to parties where I might bump into 'fallen women'?

The truth is that I inhabit a very safe little world. I just don't go to parties where 'fallen women' are to be found. Why not? Am I frightened of losing my reputation if I am seen in the 'wrong' places, with the 'wrong' people, even being touched by them? Would I be uncomfortable in the presence of such a woman? Well, I guess I might be. I might be embarrassed, unsure of myself and my reactions, unsure of what other people might think of me. But if I am really so uncomfortable with fallen people, then what does that say about my own sense of righteousness? Do I need to be with 'decent' people in order to feel good about myself, to feel 'holy'? Of course, it is threatening to be with people whose values are very different from my own. Can I be with them, enjoy their company, even if I 'disapprove' of their lifestyle? Or am I a Pharisee really, despite all the language of grace?

If we are less welcoming than Jesus, then perhaps we have got something wrong. If part of our anxiety is a desire for visible respectability, then perhaps we have not really grasped 'justification by faith alone' or even the loving grace of God. There is an extravagance and an untidiness here which is typical of God, but less typical of the historical Church. We have the chance to be different, but it requires a change in us. It requires a Lutheran sense that we too are at the same time still sinful, as well as justified by God. If somewhere, deep inside us, we have this sense of continual gratitude to a God who always reaches out to us, then that will enable us to be pastorally gentle and welcoming to the unrespectable, even fallen women...

QUESTIONS FOR REFLECTION AND DISCUSSION

1. What sort of people do you have as your friends? What sort of people do you not have as your friends? Why?
2. What sort of person would you honestly find it difficult to see walking into your church this coming Sunday? Perhaps, in your mind's eye, picture Jesus welcoming them warmly. How does this make you feel?
3. What would help your church to be the sort of place where 'unrespectable' people would feel welcome?

✤

TELL ME ABOUT YOUR GOD, THEN!

Luke 10: 38–42

The training for the pastoral team was going well. Confidence and trust had been growing throughout the weeks, and people seemed very willing to share openly about themselves and their feelings. They were a wonderful group of warm, caring people, who were genuinely enthusiastic about serving their local community in every way that they could. Then we hit a rock! We were discussing the fact that when we visit as representatives of the church we may be asked to speak about God. I was not thinking of encouraging the group to use the pastoral situation as a means of steering the conversation towards God, as that would be a grave misuse of the situation. What I meant was that when we visit people in need they may well have questions about God that they might legitimately want to ask of us, as God's followers:

'Why did my son have to die so young? It just isn't fair. He was a good lad and never did anyone any harm.'

'Why has my elderly mother got to suffer all the pain and humiliation of this long, drawn-out death? I can't imagine a God who could allow such a thing.'

'Where is my husband now? Do you think he's in heaven? He never went to church much, but he did believe in God and he was a good man.'

'I'm so unhappy since my husband left me. I feel so depressed I often think that I can't go on.'

'All this God stuff's OK, but I just can't forgive my wife for what she did to me!'

In short, I was talking about all those difficult questions around the issue of why bad things happen to good people. Well, I may as well have lit the blue touchpaper and stood back! You could feel the discomfort in the air, and finally one lady exploded. She slammed her Filofax down on her lap and said: 'Well, if you're expecting me to talk about God to the people I visit, you can count me out!' And, to my astonishment, everyone nodded in agreement. I wondered what exactly was going on here. Gradually, I teased it out of them that they were absolutely terrified of talking to people about their faith because they thought their lack of theological knowledge would be found out. And all this from a group of people, most of whom had been going to church nearly all their lives.

I went home perplexed and wondering how to get through this hiccup the following week. I racked my brains for a way to encourage them to think that they could do it. As I drove home through their beautiful village, looking at the gardens in the late evening sun, I suddenly thought 'growing roses'. The next week I told them this story:

Supposing you grew roses in your garden, and a new person moved into the area and came to live next door to you. He wanted to grow roses and, seeing over the wall that you grew roses, asked you for a bit of advice about what grows well in this village. 'Of course I'm no expert,' you would probably say, 'but I've been growing roses here for many years. Now that one over there is hopeless; the petals blow off in the slightest breeze, and that one has never really flourished, but those two over there always do really well. They're a feast of colour for months and the scent is wonderful, especially in the evening.' Can you imagine saying instead: 'No, I'm afraid I'm not an expert on roses, and I can't give you any advice, even though I've been growing roses for years in this village. If you need help, I suggest you go down to see the chap at the garden centre.'

This is exactly what we are required to do when people ask us about God. Of course the first point is that, in effect, they have to look over your fence and notice that you 'grow roses', that there is something significant and different about your life. That certainly gives me pause for thought! Then they ask you to do the same as in the rose-growing story, in other words, to share your experience to date of knowing God. OK, you're no expert but what is your experience so far? Mostly, that is all people want to know, but if you should get entangled in deep theological questions, you have recourse to the expert—not the garden centre, but the local vicar!

When explained in this way, the whole issue suddenly seemed to be within the group's grasp. They could see how they could talk about their experience to date just as it was: no perfect answers but nonetheless their experience of God in their lives.

The Gospel story of Jesus with Martha and Mary can challenge us in this way. It points out the difference between the two women, the contrast between doing for Jesus and being with him. It seems to me that we are often better at doing things for God than we are at speaking about him. However, at the end of the day, whatever service we can offer is of much less importance for people than coming to their own faith in God. It is a bit like finding a huge store of food and generously handing it out to people but never actually telling people where the food is, so that they can find it for themselves. Works without words are only a partial gift.

The other crucial thing that Mary got right was spending time both talking to and listening to Jesus. It was time which enabled her to get to know him and to gain from him all that he wanted to offer. We know well enough that if we don't give time to people we never really know them, never really come to appreciate them and never come to love them. When you are deeply in love you cannot bear being apart from the beloved and struggle so hard not to speak of them. Their name is always on your lips. Would that we knew Jesus that well and loved him that much!

Years ago, when my son was little, I had a friend with a girl the same age as my son, and we used to while away many an afternoon in each other's company. She was a left-wing atheist, and a charming, intelligent, kind and generous person. She knew I was a Christian but it seemed that we had agreed to differ. Then one afternoon, sitting in the hot sun in some beautiful gardens near Oxford, beginning to eat our ice-creams with our tired children, she said to me 'Tell me about your God, then!' I wanted to say that it was too hot; I was too tired; I needed time to think, anything except do what she asked. But I knew that this was my moment and it would not easily come again, so in my hesitant way I began to share with her what I knew of Jesus and my experience of him. It felt so inadequate, so inexpert, so badly formed and I don't know what she really made of it—except that I remember her saying that she had never heard of God spoken of like that, and she found him rather attractive!

QUESTIONS FOR REFLECTION AND DISCUSSION

1. Do you think people would see that you are 'growing roses'? What experience of 'growing roses' would you share?
2. Mary was willing to spend time with Jesus to get to know him well. Reflect upon the time you are willing to spend with Jesus, or are you rather more of a Martha? How do we get this balance right?
3. How would you answer the challenge: 'Tell me about your God, then'?

✛

EVANGELISM AS SPIRITUAL CONVERSATION

John 4:1–30, 39–42

These days it's cool to have a personal trainer: someone who gives advice and guidance on such aspects of life as exercise, time management and lifestyle issues. There is also a growing awareness of the spiritual dimension of life, though for most people Church and Christianity would be the last places they would think of looking for help in this sphere.

They might, however, think of going to see a spiritual director: someone to whom they could talk about spiritual concerns and who would explore with them spiritual issues to do with God, their inner lives and possibly their personal values. In other words, a sort of personal spiritual trainer. A spiritual director may be seen as independent of the institution of the Church, a person who will keep confidentiality, and who has some knowledge of faith plus some skills which may be helpful along the way. If life is a journey, then it makes good sense to have a companion with whom to travel. Seen in this light, spiritual direction could be a valuable tool of evangelism. It is not a form of counselling or psychotherapy but, like them, it offers a safe, non-judgmental place where people can explore and articulate their deepest thoughts and longings. More-over, in our therapy-centred world, it provides a Christian response to the pursuit of individualism and narcissism which clouds what being truly human is about.

There are numerous good examples of spiritual directors

throughout the history of the Church, and today there is a widespread revival of the practice across the different Christian traditions. To gain insight into the best kind of practice, however, we need simply to return to the Gospels and study the way Jesus dealt with the people he encountered in his earthly ministry. The example of Jesus and the woman of Samaria in John chapter 4 demonstrates how he met with individuals right where they were and took them seriously, but did not leave them there. His aim was that they might know God as he knew God, and the aim of all spiritual direction is to point people further towards God and help them discover their own journey of faith.

In the story of Jesus' encounter with the Samaritan woman, he sought to help her gain the self-knowledge she needed to become what she was meant to be. He did this by enabling her to discover her own thirst for God. There is no doubt that she had an interest in spiritual matters. Indeed, she was eager to tell Jesus what she knew and engage him in intellectual debate (compare vv. 9, 12, 19–20). Many people today may talk about spiritual things, while shying away from personal commitment. But spiritual direction is personal. It is not about knowledge or academic debate, and Jesus prevented the woman from going off on a tangent, thereby avoiding the real work which the Holy Spirit wanted to do in her (vv 13–15, 21).

In the encounters of spiritual direction, there are always three people involved: director, directee and the Holy Spirit, who is the real director. There is no direct mention of the Holy Spirit here, but he is implicit in the symbol of the water, which moves the discussion from the realm of the physical to the spiritual and is offered to the woman as a free gift (vv. 13–15). It is the task of director and directee to listen to the Spirit together so that both are engaged in the work of discernment.

The woman seems to have been seeking spiritual truth, although at the time of her meeting with Jesus she had not planned for such revelations concerning either God or her own private life. Like many people today, she could not be called a conventional believer but she had sufficient interest in spiritual matters to allow a discussion to take place. Similarly, many who go to see a spiritual director do their best to avoid the real issue by talking about all kinds of other interesting but irrelevant topics. People are not always aware of what the real issue is. Typically, they think it lies in knowledge, or that they can somehow remain detached from its implications in their own lives. The woman may have tried to distract Jesus with academic questions, because she sensed that he could discern her true self and thus felt uncomfortably close to being exposed for what she really was. Like any good director, however, Jesus was not looking to make her appear foolish, only to help her to face up to what was preventing her spiritual freedom and growth. He began with a simple and direct question, (v. 7), but soon brought the subject round to the real issue, (v. 10), and when the woman did not get the point (v. 11), persisted with what was important (vv. 13–14). The conversation begins with a very practical request for a drink, but quickly moves on from the physical to the spiritual.

The woman is unlikely to have intended bringing up the subject of her relationships with men, so Jesus gave her an invitation to be honest about her situation with his direct command (v. 16). He graciously allows her next 'red herring' about where worship should take place to become part of the conversation which is to lead her further towards the truth (vv. 19–24). He confronts her with the truth about herself but puts it in a way which speaks to her need. She discovers herself truly known and yet still accepted, and this sets her free to know herself and therefore be herself.

Instead of being affronted at his knowledge of her private life, she finds his frankness liberating and goes off to tell her neighbours about her meeting with Jesus. Who can he be?

Spiritual direction has a role in the evangelistic mission of the Church because it is never solely for the benefit of the recipient. The Christian life is not meant to be a cosy vertical relationship between myself and God. It must have horizontal repercussions, practical consequences affecting the way I live. The woman returned to her town and invited people to come and meet Jesus. They came and many believed for themselves (vv. 39–42) because they saw the difference Jesus had made to her.

QUESTIONS FOR REFLECTION AND DISCUSSION

1. Look again at how Jesus introduced the concept of living water into the conversation. Can you recall an instance of an occasion when something ordinary and everyday led on to a conversation about spiritual issues? What other examples of everyday experience might we use to engage people in conversation about the Christian faith?
2. What are the main principles of spiritual direction seen in this passage which could be helpful to the task of evangelism? Can you think of other encounters in the Gospels which also illustrate the work of spiritual direction?
3. In her book *Holy Listening* (DLT, 1992), Margaret Guenther describes spiritual direction using three metaphors: midwife, teacher and giver of hospitality. Which best describes Jesus in his encounter with the Samaritan woman?

✛

Section Three

THE EARLIEST CHURCHES IN EVANGELISM

The oldest parts of the New Testament writings are the letters to the earliest churches. Along with the history of the church in the book of Acts, they give us many insights into the way the first Christians went about evangelizing after the death and resurrection of Jesus and the giving of the Spirit at Pentecost. The book of Acts provides numerous passages for reflection. The ones we have chosen include some well-known ones, such as the enigmatic encounter between Philip and the Ethiopian eunuch (Acts 8:26–40). The practice of hospitality in evangelism is picked up from the story of Paul and Silas in Philippi (Acts 16:6–15) and a number of other Acts passages are treated in imaginative ways.

The final selections are all from the letters of Paul, and draw out theological themes important for evangelism (for example, how we find God in creation—Romans 1:19–20) and some practical ideas (for example, Philippians 2).

Once again, this is just a selection from many possible passages. As you read the letters to the first churches, we encourage you to look out for evangelistic themes—how does this concern relate to sharing the good news? Is there an insight about God here which is important to share with other people? Can we see an evangelistic method which we could learn from?

❖

PHILIP AND THE EUNUCH: THE EASE AND CHALLENGE OF WITNESS

Acts 8:26–40

The story of Philip sharing the good news with the Ethiopian eunuch helps us to consider how it may sometimes feel easy and natural to witness to our faith, and how it may sometimes be challenging and demanding.

EASY FOR HIM

In the first place, no one could have had it easier than Philip. If ever there was a prime opportunity for evangelism, Philip had it. He overhears a stranger reading aloud from the scriptures (v. 30), and only has to say: 'Do you know what Isaiah is on about?' to be invited into a comfy chariot (v. 31).

He doesn't even have to start the conversation once he's there; instead, the official questions him about the text. And it's an easy question; it's not one of those questions like: 'Well, if God's so loving, how come he commanded Joshua to massacre all the inhabitants of Jericho once the walls had fallen down?' Instead, the Ethiopian eunuch asks: 'This suffering servant Isaiah's talking about, who is it?' (vv. 32–34).

When Philip has told the stranger about Jesus, he doesn't have to shepherd him carefully towards a weekly meeting where, in a welcoming environment, he can gradually explore more about the

Christian faith and overcome his uncertainty about church, until, by the end of the course he is ready to make his own commitment. Instead, the eunuch interrupts Philip (v. 36) to say: 'Look, there's some water! Why not baptize me?'

EASY FOR US

So, you may say, 'That was lucky for Philip, but during the Queen's recent visit to Durham, I didn't overhear a royal official reading the Bible aloud; I wasn't invited to join them in the limo, and no one asked me to dunk them in the River Wear.'

I grant you this precise scenario is unlikely, but I believe that we do and will have many, many opportunities in which sharing the good news about Jesus with others will feel as easy and natural and comfortable as it seemed to be for Philip.

The kind of people you are, the sort of lives you lead, can provoke questions in others, and many times your evangelism and witness will be a simple and straightforward response to the questions of those you are alongside.

HARD FOR HIM AND FOR US

From one point of view, Philip seems to have had an easy time as an evangelist, and there are times when it will feel easy for us, too. From another perspective, however, Philip's story illustrates the challenge and demand of being a witness to Christ. Here are three aspects of the story that show the difficulty of the task he faced.

TAKING THE INITIATIVE

Philip had to take the first step. He saw this grand official in his chariot, in charge of the entire treasury of the queen of Ethiopia (v. 27) (Ethiopia was the name for a region now within southern

Egypt) and presumably he was nervous about approaching such an august personage. He did not know at that point that the eunuch was reading Isaiah, and so he would have had little optimism that he would receive a sympathetic hearing.

Nevertheless, in obedience to the Spirit (v. 29), he ran up to the chariot and interrupted the eunuch's reading with a question that is almost impertinent: 'Do you understand what you are reading?' (v. 30).

So the chain of happy events that leads to the official's baptism do not take place by themselves, but are set off by Philip's obedient initiative following the Spirit's request. The events seem amenable to God's purposes, but only once Philip has obediently become part of them.

One of the challenges of evangelism, then, is attending to the Spirit, and being prepared at the appropriate time to take an initiative that we may be nervous about. Occasionally, as we do so, we may receive the strong and rewarding sense of being part of God's purposes, just as Philip did.

TALKING TO EVERYONE

Philip didn't only take the initiative in talking to someone, but took the initiative in talking to a very strange person. The Ethiopian eunuch was not like him.

First, he was probably a Gentile, at a time when only Jews were Christians. We know the ructions that shook the church later when it had to face the policy question of admitting Gentiles (Acts 15).

Second, he was probably literally a eunuch, a castrated male. Although the Greek word *eunouchos* could also refer to a high official who was not castrated, it is unlikely that an uncastrated male could hold high office in a queen's court.

Eunuchs must have been shocking to Jews like Philip. Eunuchs were not permitted to belong to the nation of Israel, nor were they allowed to minister in the sanctuary (Deuteronomy 23:1).

So here was Philip, faced with someone very strange indeed, a

Gentile eunuch, and yet he overcomes all his fear of strangeness to speak clearly of Jesus to him.

Think for a moment: who would be as strange and discomfiting to you as a Gentile eunuch was to Philip? How would you talk about Jesus to them? Perhaps a transsexual is the best comparison. Sometimes the demand of evangelism will be to talk to people very different to us, to make the imaginative leap that Jesus died even for them.

Maybe Philip remembered the prophecy in Isaiah 56 that even the eunuch and the foreigner would be delivered (Isaiah 56:4–8).

THINKING THROUGH THE MESSAGE

Philip had a hard job because he had to take the initiative in obedience to the Spirit, and he had to share the good news about Jesus with someone very strange to him.

His witness was also difficult because he had to think afresh about the message he gave to the eunuch. The eunuch was reading from Isaiah's depiction of the suffering servant, in Isaiah 53. The use of this prophecy to refer to Christ has become commonplace for us, but Philip may have been the first to link the suffering servant with Jesus.

If so, he had to think hard not only about how to approach the Ethiopian eunuch, and about the foreignness of this individual, but also how to relate what the eunuch was trying to understand with the good news about Jesus Christ. Could it be that this familiar prophecy had become realized in the person of Jesus Christ? Of course! Once he had made the connection, it was obvious.

Evangelism is challenging because we also have to rethink how we tell the good news about Jesus in different contexts. How are we to make connections with the people we want to talk to? What are they reading, or watching, that we can use to make a bridge between them and the gospel?

Whether it is *Harry Potter* or the *Star Wars* series, we are often required to think anew about making connections, just as Philip did.

OUR WORK AS GOD'S WORK

From one perspective, Philip had a golden opportunity to witness to Christ, and sometimes our opportunities will fall just as easily to us. From another perspective, Philip's job was tough: he had to overcome his fear of taking the initiative, of talking to someone very strange, of telling the gospel story in a new way, and there will be times when we will need to face these challenges too.

What strikes me finally about this story, though, is the work of God throughout: it's an angel that tells Philip to go to Gaza, the Spirit that tells him to approach the chariot, and the same Spirit that snatches Philip away at the end and takes him to Azotus (vv. 39–40). In our sharing of the good news about Jesus, may we take confidence from the truth that whether our work is easy or challenging, we are instruments of God's purposes, and our success will depend not on our own capacities, but on God's power and will.

QUESTIONS FOR REFLECTION AND DISCUSSION

1. In what contexts do you find sharing your faith easy?
2. When do you find it hard to share your faith?
3. What resources might be helpful in overcoming this difficulty, either from this passage or elsewhere?

❖

PICTURES OF SALVATION: EVANGELISM IN PHILIPPI

Acts 16:11–40

In Acts 16, Luke tells the story of the preaching of the gospel in the Roman colony of Philippi. It is a story of the Christian gospel crossing boundaries. Thus far, Paul and his companions have preached the good news in Cyprus and modern Turkey. Now they are led by the Holy Spirit to cross into Europe. For the first time, the small group of disciples address the question of where to begin in a city which has no synagogue. Here we find Jews preaching to Gentiles, men addressing women, East speaking to West.

Luke constructs his story of what happened in Philippi around a series of related incidents. In the first, Paul and his companions preach at a place of prayer and Lydia is converted and baptized (16:11–15). In the second, Paul delivers a slave girl from a spirit of divination (16:16–18). Her owners complain and, as a result of that complaint, Paul and Silas are arrested and put in prison (16:19–24). During the night, there is an earthquake. Instead of escaping, Paul and Silas remain and witness to the jailer, who, like Lydia, is baptized with all his household (16:25–34). At the end of the chapter, Paul and Silas confront their accusers, who have thrown them into prison without charge, and receive an apology. The disciples depart from Philippi with honour, taking their leave of the young Christian community which is now gathered in Lydia's home (16:35–40).

Like all of Luke's narrative, it is possible to read the account of evangelism in Philippi at a number of different levels. It is certainly possible to draw some valuable lessons for a strategy for evangelism and evangelists from the story of Lydia and the jailer. The pattern followed by Paul in Philippi bears a marked resemblance to the instructions given by Jesus to the 72 in Luke 10:1–9. When bringing the gospel to a new community, Luke commends the strategy of finding those who are most responsive and clearly intends us to understand that we will discover such people in the most likely situations (a place of prayer) and the most unlikely (a prison cell). We learn that the Spirit is already at work in the lives of those to whom the gospel is proclaimed and in bringing together the evangelist and those who are ready to listen. We learn (as often in Acts) that the early Christians are unashamed entrepreneurs, making the most of every opportunity and adversity as a space to communicate their message.

Luke also invites us to read a little deeper into the text. Here and elsewhere in Acts, the author explores a range of different metaphors or pictures of salvation through what seems to be a deliberate and subtle selection of particular language and themes. There is no single or preferred way in Luke to describe becoming a Christian or the way of responding to the Christian gospel. Instead, many different and wonderful facets of salvation are explored through the way the story is told. Two linked themes are found in the story of the gospel in Philippi.

OPEN HEARTS—OPEN HOMES

The first is the profound image of welcome and hospitality, particularly the hospitality of the heart. Luke uses the metaphor of the opening of the heart to describe Lydia's response to Paul's preaching (Acts 16:15). The picture is found elsewhere in the New Testament, especially in John's Gospel ('We will come to them and make our home with them' in John 14:23) and in Revelation ('Listen! I am standing at the door, knocking' in Revelation 3:20). In the Philippi narrative, Lydia's open heart is linked explicitly with the offer of actual hospitality to Paul and the companions: 'If you have judged me to be faithful to the Lord, come and stay at my home' (16:15). Nowhere else in Acts is such an invitation recorded. The theme is extended into the encounter with the jailer. We see Paul and Silas 'enjoying' one kind of hospitality from the jailer at the beginning of the story as 'he put them in the innermost cell and fastened their feet in the stocks' (16:24). The sign of the jailer's conversion is a different kind of hospitality altogether: 'He brought them up into the house and set food before them; and he and his entire household rejoiced that he had become a believer in God' (16:34). At the centre of the jailer's conversion is the wonderful picture of double 'washing' which, again, is linked to the theme of gracious hospitality (and the story of the foot-washing): 'At the same hour of the night he took them and washed their wounds; then he and his entire family were baptized without delay' (16:33). We return to the image again at the end of the story, where Paul and Silas return to Lydia's home (16:40) before leaving the city.

RELEASE TO THE CAPTIVES

The prophecy from Isaiah quoted by Jesus in the synagogue in Nazareth provides much of the 'shape' for the telling of the good news both in the Gospel of Luke and in Acts (Luke 4:18–19). The theme of captives being set free is explored and reinforced in Acts by the three accounts of the early Christians being physically set free from prison (you will find the others in Acts 5:17–21 and 12:6–11). The theme is linked much more directly to salvation in this chapter by Luke's telling of the remarkable story of the jailer. Paul and Silas are imprisoned yet still able to praise God and speak of the gospel (16:25). They and their fellow prisoners are liberated by the earthquake, yet stay where they are. The jailer himself perceives that they were captive yet free and are now free yet captive. His response is the deliberately ambiguous cry: 'Sirs, what must I do to be saved?' (v. 30). We are meant to understand that at the end of the passage freedom has come not only to Paul and Silas but to the jailer and his whole household. The Christian gospel is a means of liberation and leads to freedom.

An important lesson from the story is the encouragement to explore a wider range of the biblical pictures of salvation in our reflection on evangelism, instead of simply the ones which are the most familiar in our own tradition or story. Both the theme of hospitality and the theme of freedom have played an important role in the Christian tradition of singing about salvation in well-known hymns and choruses, but not so much in testimony and preaching.

QUESTIONS FOR REFLECTION AND DISCUSSION

1. Can you think of hymns, songs or pictures which use the images of hospitality or of liberation to express the truths of Christian conversion?
2. How would you tell your own story using the picture of hospitality or the picture of liberation?

✤

MOVING OUT TO MOVE ON: EVANGELISM WRESTLING WITH BELIEF AND BUILDINGS

Acts 19:8–10

One Sunday evening my local Anglican congregation built a church. We had been doing some Bible study on what it might mean to be church and then we went 'hands on'. Into the space in the middle of the floor we piled a variety of cardboard boxes, and out of them emerged a surprisingly solid and impressive construction.

There was a general air of satisfaction with this collaborative outcome, until one bewildered participant observed that he could not see a door.

'But there is a door,' someone confidently asserted from the other side of the room, 'and if you were sitting where I am sitting you would see it'.

There followed a thoughtful silence before this robust response: 'That may be so, but from where I'm sitting there's no way into this church. And, incidentally, there's no way out, either!'

The chilling clarity of that observation continues to haunt my thinking about evangelism in a local church setting.

- Can the Church hold as prisoner within its walls those who would move on in the ministry of evangelism?
- Does the Church stifle and destroy that which it is called to share?
- How do we wrestle with constraint and conflict, and work to shift perspectives and open up Christian experience?

111

As the story of Acts 19:8–10 unfolds, our attention is drawn to evangelistic questions around belief and buildings—how to move out and on in sharing the gospel.

Paul has returned to Ephesus, picking up where he left off—at the synagogue (v. 8). Who could be better positioned to open up the good news of Jesus than God's own people? Here Paul finds a welcome, an accepted set of beliefs and assumed common ground. Staying within its confines could prove a safe option; breaking out of its confines with a different perspective and mission focus could prove unpopular.

Undeterred in his evangelistic focus, we find that Paul 'spoke out boldly' and 'argued persuasively about the kingdom of God' (v. 8). 'The kingdom of God' is not a common theme in Acts. Such a radical reinterpretation of traditional Jewish belief made it a particularly contentious topic and, anyway, the Ephesians thought they had a hold on the kingdom of God. They were not looking to revise their views. Paul's handling of the scriptures questioned their assumptions, exposed their prejudices and eroded the bedrock of their thinking.

The mould of synagogue tradition was broken by the need to look again at belief, to re-visit scripture, and to decide what—and who— is at the heart of faith. Paul rigorously blazed the trail for a life-transforming relationship with Jesus. And people had to respond.

Someone recently said to me: 'I've always found going to church a comfort—but all these clerical scandals have shaken my faith. I don't know what to believe anymore.'

The comfort zone of her belief was shaken, and we thought about possible outcomes:

• Staying in a place of confusion and disillusionment, with probable loss of faith.
• Denying that belief is being challenged, with loss of spiritual integrity.
• Revisiting the Jesus of scripture to open up new understanding, with potential spiritual growth.

She warmed to the latter but commented sadly: 'Folks in my church don't like their ignorance to be exposed and addressed—it makes for too much awkwardness and hard work.'

Opening up new doors can be messy and tough. The gospel is not easily accommodated, and it always necessitates change. Challenging assumptions and prejudices of belief can open up churches to engage with the experience of 21st-century life with enlarged perspectives. Paul's ministry demonstrates the patience, rigour and risk involved in tackling comfort zones of belief.

Have we the boldness and the courage to look ourselves at the disturbing story of Jesus in scripture and then present him to others? Dare we open up and release God's people from within the Church into new explorations of belief?

It may be a rough ride. It proved so for Paul. There were those within the synagogue who did not like being confronted with challenges to their beliefs. They were difficult, resistant and malicious, and were making more noise than the disciples who chose the way of Jesus.

By the end of three persistent months, the confrontation and constraints within the synagogue were making it impossible for Paul to further the work of evangelism (v. 9). The doors of the building closed inwards, and the gospel was trapped.

For Paul, the time had come to move out of the building so as to move on with the Church's primary calling of evangelism. He took with him those who had committed themselves to the way of Jesus (v. 9). He did not set up a rival church, but found a more accessible centre for sharing the faith—the lecture hall of the philosopher Tyrannus (v. 10).

It was a bold move to embark on Christian discussion groups during the sleepy heat of the day—but by the grace of God and the spiritual energy of the co-evangelists, it worked. The doors in and out of the hall of Tyrannus were many: 'This went on for two years, so that all the Jews and Greeks who lived in the province of Asia heard the word of the Lord' (v. 10, NIV).

We are not told how many responded to these presentations and discussions by making a decision for Christ; what mattered in evangelistic terms was that the opportunity to engage at length with the gospel was made freely available to all. And when the task was complete, Paul moved on; the hall of Tyrannus had served its purpose.

How and where can the church reach the community with the gospel? What if, as was Paul's experience, there are those within who are difficult, resistant, even malicious, who make more noise than those who want to open up the good news?

One response is to move out of the building physically. Paul experimented with a meeting place where the Christian faith could be offered and explored with a freedom and accessibility not possible in a religious building.

A church of cardboard boxes could never have been built in the formal and traditional constraints of nave and sanctuary. We were in an alternative setting—a community hall normally used for toddler and after-school groups. Like the hall of Tyrannus, it was a place where people had an opportunity to meet Jesus outside the Church's terms. From time to time, we have returned for similar experimental activities and outreach.

Paul's example challenges the Church today to open up the doors of our belief to accommodate the Jesus of scripture, and then to open up the doors of our buildings to share what we have experienced. It is a costly calling, and it will be resisted, but the message is clear—move out to move on.

QUESTIONS FOR REFLECTION AND DISCUSSION

1. What disturbs the comfort zones of belief in my experience of church life? How might I work with the disturbance to create an opportunity for evangelism? *
2. Who are the people in my church with a vision to open up new doors? How might we together prayerfully search out ways of moving out to move on in evangelism?

3. What are the possible buildings and activities in my locality where people could have an opportunity to meet Jesus outside the church's terms?

⁜

ENCOURAGING THE EVANGELISTS

Acts 20:13–38

Dear Paul,

It was so good to see you last week, and I hope the journey back to Jerusalem is not proving too eventful. I was a little hurt when you didn't actually come to Ephesus. We were looking forward to hosting you, and then John wanted to take you out for lunch; the young people wanted you to speak at their meeting; Martha wasn't feeling too well and I thought you could just call in on her, and then we had arranged for you to meet some of the city officials, and you could have had some time for yourself—we had arranged some sightseeing with a few friends, who were eager to talk to you. Never mind, I am sure you had your reasons for suggesting that only the elders came to meet you at Miletus.

I write because what you said really challenged me. I feel the Lord might be asking me to be an evangelist. The aqueduct business is quite fluid at the moment, and although there is plenty of bread to be made on the markets, I want to be serious about God's call.

To be honest, I can't remember all that you said, but a number of things stayed with me. In fact, you seem to know all the right things to say. I trust you because I know you. Some of these teleological evangelists just pop in with their programmes to transform our churches and you get the impression that the offering is more important to them than we are. You were different, and that's why we took you to our heart. But not only that, you gave us confidence. It struck me at Miletus that you reminded us that the Holy Spirit called us just as he called you. I wasn't sure about it when you first said it because I'm not really into riots, mobs, prison or thorns in the flesh (by the way, what did you mean by that?). But you recognized us and believed in us enough to trust us with the church. It's a bit of a risk—especially with You Know Who as treasurer! Thank you for including us.

When you spoke of your ministry of proclaiming repentance and faith to all, it reminded me how often I overcomplicate the gospel. I get tied up with minor details and secondary issues and find myself spending hours with my friends debating Homer without ever mentioning Jesus. Then I remember that Jesus has changed around my life, and he can do it for anybody. My Aunt Pat was such a pain that I thought she would never come into our church. Then she just turned up out of the blue saying she had had an 'experience'. Knowing her background, I didn't want to ask which one! To be honest, Paul, she never heard you preach but she seems to know Jesus and is certainly growing. I wonder how she heard?

If I do become an evangelist, will I go through what you go through? I was in tears when you spoke about what will happen, and told us that we won't see you again. But I do feel driven by the Spirit in the way you described. I'm not sure that I could say that my life is of no value. Did you mean that, and is it something you come to in a moment or gradually? I do want to work for the Lord. I want to be accountable to him rather than to my mother's plan for my career. But I do have responsibilities here with the family. Dad is not too well and the kids are young. What do you suggest?

That bit about being on guard came at just the right time. We had this bloke preaching last week—well, it didn't sound right. I mean, he was very good, with some brilliant Moses jokes, and he didn't even use notes. Lots of people in the church were raving about him, and a few were saying that he doesn't go on as long as you used to. I mean, they had a point—11am to 4pm every day for two years in the Hall of Tyrannus was a long sermon! I couldn't place what was wrong with this bloke, but there was something that didn't ring true. It was all about health and wealth. I need to know the whole story of God's revelation if I am going to be able to look after the church. That scares me. How can I do it by myself?

I feel overwhelmed by it all at times. How can I preach a message which has the power to change lives? How can I face the sacrifice of time, reputation and even my own life and remain faithful to what we have received? I do need to guard myself but the lesson I really took away was how you commended us to God and the message of his grace. My friend Donna says that God's grace means his extravagant generosity. I know that he saves me and empowers me—even in the face of Aunt Pat. Grace gives me optimism about the future. I like that—do you think that some of your theologian friends might use it?

We are going to miss you so much. You Know Who sends his regards, and a query about the fact that you never claimed your mileage. I feel sad, but we can do it without you—because God is with us.

I commend you to his grace!

Grace and peace to you,

Ty

QUESTIONS FOR REFLECTION AND DISCUSSION

1. How would you respond to Ty's questions if you were Paul?
2. What four insights would you have taken away if you had been in Paul's audience?

❖

WHERE IS GOD TO BE FOUND?

Romans 1:20

When someone dies, all we have left after their passing is their possessions. It is a painful process to sift through the home of a loved one and decide what to keep in their memory and what to pass on to the local charity shop. Someone's home and its store of earthly treasure reveals a great deal about a person, their tastes, their interests, what they value and what gives them pleasure. I recall visiting my grandmother's home on the day of her funeral, and the smell, the furniture, the numerous knick-knacks and pictures in the house brought about what can only be described as a rekindling of her presence. This was the home she had created and the variety of gathered possessions enabled me to realize and experience this loving woman who no longer exists in a physical body. What we create embodies something of the essence of who we are.

This verse from the letter to the Romans tells us something about the way God makes his divine love and mercy known through his creation, through the material, physical world. It is about how God is revealed and experienced in the world. God exists as Spirit, but we need to acknowledge the fact that the Spirit requires embodiment so that it can be realized and known. Paul makes this point by saying that all creation bears God's fingerprints. God can be known through his creation. This is the way in which his wisdom, power and generous love can be experienced by humanity.

When Paul wrote these words, the gospel was known by only a fraction of the world's population, and what follows concerning the wickedness of humankind and their suppression of the truth is not

119

only about all those who have heard the gospel and rejected it, but all of humanity (vv. 18, 19). What he says is based upon the story of Adam and points to the experience of the whole human race. The problem with which the passage wrestles at this point is that nature, the whole created world, shows us that there is a God. What other explanation can there be? But humanity rejects or denies this and makes itself a god. According to Paul, we are without excuse. Twice (vv. 19, 21) he says that God can be known, but instead of glorifying God, worship is given to false gods and idols created by humanity.

How does this verse connect with mission, evangelism and the Church? It tells us something important about revelation and incarnation. It points us to the truth that what God creates carries his Spirit, and within this physical material world and through the material things of life we can gain glimpses of him and engage with his spiritual presence. This can be stretched further and applied to human beings too. As people made in the image of God, we are bearers of his Spirit, and through us his Spirit may be found. Of course, the supreme example of this is found in Christ, who was in every sense the embodied presence of God in a specific time and place.

The mission of the Church has to be focused on enabling God to be known by humanity, through his creation and through us as created beings. We, as the Church, the body of Christ, are members of a community, which is called to bear witness to God's continuing presence in the world. The community of the Church exists to be true to this vocation: to be the place where God is found and his power and nature realized as a living presence. This is a calling, to enable people to find God in this physical, material world. I believe this is at the heart of our mission as the Church. It holds the responsibility to be where God's presence can be realized or, as Helen Oppenheimer puts it: 'The church is there to make God findable'[11] and 'God's people... have the greater but hopeful responsibility of being the presence, the findability, of God upon earth'.[12]

So when Paul writes that God's eternal power and divine nature can be clearly seen from what has been created, he is pointing to this very idea of the findability of God. As Christians, we should be immersed in this very business of making the divine love and mercy of God a real presence in people's lives, enabling them to find God and understand more of him through our part in the body of Christ. This is a significant part of the work of the evangelist, an awesome responsibility. As we consider the present state of the Church, with all of its divisions, declining membership and many flaws, it is perhaps difficult to find God's presence within it. However, it is not the Church's history that necessarily enables it to be the place where God is found; it is what it affirms concerning the truth about God: that God is faithful to his people, and God is love. We, as fallen human beings, make up the Church but are called as bearers of his Spirit to reveal his presence.

The history of the Church, with its continued struggle to enable Christians to go on experiencing the God of mercy and love in their lives and sharing this with those who desire to know God, gives us confidence in the findability of God within this imperfect institution. What it has to do is proclaim with conviction and enthusiasm, in a relevant and accessible way, the living presence of God in the world. This is part of our evangelistic task, but it is not done in our own strength; we are not independent operators in this mission. As the body of Christ is made up of many parts, all dependent on each other, so the body is ultimately dependent on God's Spirit working through and in each one of us. It is the community of the Church that bears witness to the continuing presence of God. As evangelists, we are called to enable others to find God and make his presence a reality in their lives.

QUESTIONS FOR REFLECTION AND DISCUSSION

1. Reflect upon how God's presence is made known to you through creation.
2. How can the Church enable others to realize God's presence in the world?

⁘

THE WORK OF AN EVANGELIST:
PICTURES IN 1 CORINTHIANS

1 Corinthians 3:1–17

How do you picture the work of an evangelist? What images come to mind? Perhaps a man standing on a soapbox on the street corner with people walking past, embarrassed? Perhaps someone at the front of a church preaching to the congregation? Perhaps a couple of friends sharing their faith at the local parent and toddler group? Whatever images spring to mind, Paul invites us to think more deeply in this passage about what it means to be an evangelist. He uses three different pictures. All of them have deep biblical roots, and each of them has something to teach us about the calling to share our faith.

The context of this passage is a quarrel. The church in Corinth is beginning to divide around different issues, teachers and personalities in the early years of its life. Paul's letter seeks to build unity from beginning to end and, particularly in chapter 3, to demonstrate the way in which different teachers and personalities who have influenced the Corinthians should be related to each other and to the church there. To establish this point, Paul brings forward three of the four great biblical images of evangelism and growing in faith: the pictures of parenting, of farming and of building. The fourth great image, of the journey, is not found in this passage.

THE EVANGELIST AS A PARENT

'[I spoke to you] as infants in Christ. I fed you with milk, not solid food' (vv. 1–2).

The image of the evangelist as parent conveys a very strong and deep bond between the one who preaches the gospel and the one who responds in faith—as strong as the bond between the parent and the child. Responsible evangelism, then, is the very opposite of impersonal. In fact, it is one of the most deeply personal things in the world. Being actively involved in drawing another person to Christ creates a relationship of responsibility, of example, of ongoing care.

We find echoes of this image in Jesus' language of a new Christian being 'born again' (John 3:5) and in Hebrews, where this picture of new Christians needing a different form of nourishment like infants is restated (Hebrews 5:12). In the Epistles it becomes one of Paul's favourite pictures for his relationship to the disciples in all of the churches, often used with passionate expressions of love. In Galatians, Paul is like a mother in labour giving birth to her child: 'My little children, for whom I am again in the pain of childbirth until Christ is formed in you' (Galatians 4:19).

Later in 1 Corinthians, he is like a father: 'For though you might have ten thousand guardians in Christ, you do not have many fathers. Indeed, in Christ Jesus I became your father through the gospel' (1 Corinthians 4:15. See also 2 Corinthians 6:13 and 12:14).

The converse of this image is, of course, that new Christians are, in some ways, like children. They need a particular kind of care and nurture in order to grow from spiritual infancy through adolescence to maturity. That care and nurture will be about personal relationships but also about Christian teaching and discipleship. As with any parent, the person involved in evangelism will need huge stores of patience and of love. As with parenting, the relationship will normally be ongoing. In terms of Paul's main argument, he draws a distinction between the kind of teaching he gave to the Corinthians and that which they received from others at a later stage. Both kinds of teaching are important. The needs of the Christians at that stage of their development determine the teaching—it is no reflection on the wisdom of the teacher.

THE EVANGELIST AS FARMER

'I planted, Apollos watered, but God gave the growth' (v. 6).

From parenting, Paul moves to the picture of farming. Here again, he is drawing on a rich tradition of biblical imagery. The prophets speak of the word of God as like seed; of the Israelite's ploughing up the ground of their hearts (Jeremiah 4:3). Jesus himself, of course, uses farming imagery in the parables of the kingdom, most memorably in the parable of the sower and the imagery of the vine (Matthew 13:1–23 and John 15:1–11).

The farming imagery here explores two related truths which further help to build up the picture Paul is seeking to create of the relationships between the different Corinthian teachers. As with the parenting image, different work is done at different stages of the process. It has been Paul's calling to plant and Apollos' calling to water the seed. When any individual comes to faith, a range of different people are involved. Each is important and valuable but their tasks may well be very different—and, indeed, they may have different gifts. Secondly, even though there are different tasks, the growth comes from God and from God alone. The farmer (or gardener) should understand that his or her place is not to cause growth but to assist in what God is doing. It is a great privilege to be God's fellow-worker in the task.

THE EVANGELIST AS BUILDER

'According to the grace of God given to me, like a skilled master builder I laid a foundation, and someone else is building on it' (v. 10).

The image of the builder makes a similar point to the farming picture: a range of different skills and tasks are needed at each stage of the process of conversion and discipleship. For a church (or individual) to be exposed to a range of different teachers and pastors is therefore good, if not essential for its life, health and growth. Here, though, unlike the farming image, Paul does assert the priority of the one who lays the foundation. Far from being the basic, elementary work, laying the foundation is the work of the master builder (the phrase from which we take the English word 'architect'). Measuring lines, digging ditches and laying foundations is a much less glamorous part of the building task than painting the walls and hanging the pictures, but it requires immense skill. If the foundations are properly laid then it is likely that the building will remain standing for many years. The evangelist is clearly charged with laying these foundations in the gospel which is proclaimed and taught to new Christians in their earliest years. Those who build on that foundation (including, I think, the new Christians themselves) are engaged in serious work for the kingdom which will, in time, be tested by God and for which they will have to give account.

QUESTIONS FOR REFLECTION AND DISCUSSION

1. Who have been the parents, farmers and builders in your own journey of faith?
2. Which of the three images for evangelism speaks most powerfully to you and why?

❖

LIVING THE CROSS AND THE
RESURRECTION FOR OTHERS

2 Corinthians 4:7–12

In the second epistle to the Corinthian church, Paul writes an
apologetic letter in defence of his ministry. He writes to explain his
apparent weaknesses and the charge of inferiority when compared
to other apostles, whom he calls with irony 'super-apostles'. The
small paragraph of chapter 4:7–12 provides a key to understanding
Paul's defence in the light of his sense of vocation as an apostle
called to spread good news.

In verses 7–9 Paul describes his own mortal body as a clay jar. It
is something that is exceptionally fragile and yet contains a treasure.
The nature of the treasure is referred to in the preceding verse (v. 6).
It is 'the light of the knowledge of the glory of God in the face of
Jesus Christ'. This is Paul's gospel revealed in person by the Lord
Jesus Christ on the Damascus road (Acts 9:1–9). It is also his
treasure, and its light shines through his human frailty. Indeed, the
purpose of such human frailty is so that the light of the gospel and
its power might be seen clearly as coming from God alone and not
from Paul. This paradox of weakness and power sets the tone for the
subsequent verses.

These verses show us something of Paul's sense of vulnerability
and yet his clear confidence in the power of God. This is demonstrated in a series of contrasts (vv. 8–9). Paul, together with the
other apostles, is afflicted or hard pressed, perhaps even oppressed,
but he is not completely overwhelmed or crushed. In other words,

his affliction does not paralyse him. He is in difficulties, perhaps at a loss and very perplexed, but he is not yet desperate. Paul is persecuted, perhaps even pursued but, despite the attack, he is not abandoned. Indeed, it is through such experiences that Paul understands God to be faithful. Finally, Paul says that he is the one who has been cast down or struck down, but although he is knocked down he is not out for the count—he does not perish!

In these contrasts, Paul shows us something of his experience of being an apostle of the gospel of Jesus Christ. He affirms hope amid affliction and purpose amid terror, living on the edge and carrying pain. The pressure at times becomes unbearable, and yet it is precisely at this point that the power of God is made manifest. The power of God stops Paul from breaking, and more: it is at this point of supreme vulnerability that God's power is revealed through Paul to others. God has chosen to be revealed most powerfully through the frailty of human weakness and not through the alleged power of human self-confidence. In this way, glory belongs to none but God alone.

Verses 10–11 contain what are called 'parallel structures'. They are literary devices used to emphasize the point to be made. In fact, there are two different kinds of structures in these verses. At the hinge of these parallel structures in each verse is the phrase 'in order that', which means 'purpose' or 'intent'. It is through these verses that God's purpose through suffering is most clearly spelled out by Paul. The hinge helps us to understand the comparisons and contrasts within these verses.

The most important feature of both these verses is the reference to the manifestation of the life of Jesus in the weakness of human flesh. There is an identification by Paul in the death of Jesus in order that the life of Jesus, the resurrection life, might be seen clearly. This reinforces the statement of verse 7 that power is revealed in weakness. Thus, power from God is identified with the resurrection life of Jesus. It is precisely through the body of death that the life of Jesus is to be seen. Life and death are two sides of the same experience.

In verse 12, the consequence of these thoughts is announced. All this suffering, this sharing in the dying of Jesus, is for them, that is, for the Corinthians. It is because death is at work in Paul that the Corinthians experience the benefits of the gospel and resurrection life for themselves. Paul's pain means their benefit. This benefit is summed up neatly in the phrase 'the life of Jesus' (v. 11). That resurrection life touches them at Paul's expense and validates his ministry as an apostle. Whatever spiritual power they have received, it is through Paul's weakness rather than his strength.

APPLICATION

What is the significance of this passage for evangelism today? Three points of application can be suggested.

- First, this passage speaks of the Christian's identification with Jesus Christ. The life of the disciple should be modelled on the Master. Paul therefore interpreted all his experience of ministry and mission based on the key themes of death and resurrection. These experiences mark out the life of a Christian because they are central to the gospel message.
- Second, this passage speaks of hope. The gospel message offers the hope of God to a hopeless world. In the midst of pain and suffering there is Immanuel, 'God with us', and that makes all the difference in the world. This comfort is real because God changes us and empowers us in the midst of our weakness. Such strength points to the end of the age, when God will establish new heavens and a new earth, and his glory will no longer be seen in the frailty of earthen vessels but in glorified humanity.
- Third, this passage speaks of other people (vv. 11–12). There is purpose in the pain that Christians carry because the Spirit of God transforms it. Through such pain and suffering, or dying experiences, others experience the life of Jesus. How does this occur except by the Spirit of Jesus bringing the resurrection life

of Jesus to them? Evangelism is the work of God, achieved by the Spirit of God as people are brought to new birth within the kingdom of God.

QUESTIONS FOR REFLECTION AND DISCUSSION

1. Are you conscious of death and resurrection marking your own Christian life?
2. In what ways can you see the Church bringing signs of hope to the world in which we live?
3. How often do you consider the work of evangelism to be bringing the resurrection life of Jesus to others? How might this understanding affect how you do evangelism?

Part of this material has been published previously in: 'A Model of Hermeneutical Method—An Exegetical Missiological Reflection upon Suffering in 2 Corinthians 4.7–15', Evangelical Review of Theology 17.4 (1993), pp. 472–483, published by Paternoster Press.

MOTIVES IN MISSION

2 Corinthians 5:11–21

What motivates us in mission? In truth, perhaps, too many things that shouldn't:

- The guilty feeling that we ought to.
- Because it's the latest thing that growing churches are into.
- The conviction that on present trends, without mission, the future doesn't have a Church.
- Because it's part of the job; it goes with the territory.

Paul was one of the most effective and persistent missionaries of the first Christian generation. He thought and wrote more fully and more deeply than anyone in the life of the youthful new movement that sprang up among Jesus' followers. His thinking and writing were no ivory-tower business but sprang directly from his missionary praxis. What motivated him to preach Christ against all odds, in every situation, despite the cost, whatever befell him? In 2 Corinthians 5 an important window into Paul's own inner life is opened up for us. Here we see how he thought and felt about his apostolic task of turning the Gentiles to God in Christ, what motivated his mission.

Paul is writing this second letter to the Corinthians in the midst of discouragement and uncertainty. His relationship with the Corinthian church has been an up-and-down affair. By the time he writes these words, he has visited Corinth twice—once on an 18-month stay to found the church, and later on a short but disastrous visit, where he arrived and then left quickly after a sharp and painful disagreement. As he writes, the situation is on a more even keel. However, Paul felt he was misunderstood. Now he opens his heart, his inner world, to the Corinthians, so that they can understand his motives and comprehend more fully what his mission is really all about.

What motivates Paul the missionary? Not success or failure, pride or jealousy, avarice or competitiveness. The answer that Paul gives can be summed up in just two words: the gospel. The message is its own motivation. It shapes the apostle, energizing his activities and shaping his thought-world so that believing the gospel means living the gospel, and living the gospel means preaching the gospel. Of course, none of this could work for the person for whom the message of Jesus is a dead letter, a set of ideas or propositions, or just such an old, old story that it has lost its meaning, its novelty and its force. For Paul, the gospel is alive and active—the message of God's action in the life, death and resurrection of Jesus to reclaim his world, restore people to relationship with him and to bring about his reconciling purpose in human history. Again and again in these chapters, Paul explains how the magnificent sweep of God's purposes in human history captivates and shapes his life. The same God who in the beginning spoke light into existence has shone the light of Christ into our hearts (4:6). The glory of God is seen in the ministry of the new covenant (3:18). Jesus' death and resurrection is carried round every day in the lives of his ministers (4:10–12). Despite the vicissitudes of life, daily inner renewal by the Spirit is the lot of the believer (4:16). And we long for the resurrection of the body and rewards of the life to come (5:1–4). From creation, through redemption to final consummation, Paul paints a picture of how the actions of the God of all history connect to Christian living and believing.

Paul speaks of two motivations above all: the motivation of fear and the motivation of love: 'Knowing the fear of the Lord, we try to persuade others' (5:11) and 'the love of Christ urges us on' (5:14). Fear and love—what an uncomfortable pair for modern ears. How often we would like to choose between them, rejecting fear and embracing love. One is judged a poor motivation, the other a good one. But for Paul there are no such dichotomies, no such 'either—or'. Fear and love both motivate him.

It is important to be clear about what Paul means by fear and love. Paul is not speaking of the fear that sinners will go to a lost eternity, nor of the passionate love he has personally for Christ. Both were undoubtedly real to him, but both are too human-centred to be part of Paul's missionary motivation. Rather, fear and love both spring from the gospel message itself. Fear for Paul is fear of the day of accounting for himself—the day he must give an account as one who has been given a trust. The master will return. He will ask for a return on his talents. Paul will stand before the judgment seat of Jesus Christ, before the one who died as his Saviour and give account (5:10). This, and not the cross, is the end of the story, and this is part of the *denouement* to which the tale of human history is heading.

We generally judge accountability to be a good thing. Parents check that the children have done their homework. Managers review their employees' performance and in turn find themselves being held to account for their own work. The company accounts are audited to protect the shareholders. The ministers account to the church and its leaders for their work or actions. In work, home or church the unaccountable person acts purposelessly or causes damage. Accountability means purposeful action and persistence in the allotted task. Paul too knows what it is to be accountable for his actions. One day, Christ will judge and reward him for his work. This is not hellfire and damnation for the lost but appropriate accountability and reward for those arrested by the grace of God.

Nevertheless, fear without love is not enough. The love of Christ urges Paul on. It is Christ's love on the cross for Paul himself that Paul has in mind: 'We are convinced that one has died for all; therefore all have died' (5:14). In Galatians, Paul puts the same idea most dramatically and most personally: 'I have been crucified with Christ; and it is no longer I who live, but it is Christ who lives in me... who loved me and gave himself for me' (Galatians 2:19–20). Paul is overwhelmed with what Jesus has done for him. He is driven not by compassion for others but by the overwhelming sense of God's grace and Jesus' love for him. The result is a total change of life and a whole new perspective on the world. People in Christ become part of God's new creation (5:17) and in the light of Jesus' love on the cross it becomes impossible to see the people in the same old way (5:16). It is the transformation in us by God's grace and Jesus' love that opens up new vistas on the world. The world is now a place where God's reconciling purpose has been demonstrated in Christ and where every person we pass in the street is the object of Christ's reconciling love.

This is what motivates Paul to be an ambassador for Christ. The one who will judge us all has died for us and reconciled us to God. Now Paul goes in the name of Christ with the simple appeal: be reconciled to God. What motivates Paul to mission? Simply 'the gospel'. Before he was a minister of the gospel, he was the object of it. God has acted and spoken in Christ—and that action motivates and shapes the way Paul acts and speaks with others. When the message shapes the messenger, the messenger cannot help but speak.

QUESTIONS FOR REFLECTION AND DISCUSSION

1. What motivates you in mission? What holds you back from it?
2. What does it mean to you to 'fear the Lord' and to 'know the love of Christ'?

✣

A SERVANT ATTITUDE IN EVANGELISM

Philippians 2:1–11

What is our attitude in evangelism? How do we feel about sharing our faith?

- Nervous?
- Having all the answers?
- Depending on others?
- Wishing you weren't on your own?
- Wishing you were on your own?

The reality is a whole spectrum of attitudes, and that's just me!

How do we cope when reality does not match our expectations and attitudes?

A friend of mine was taking part in a weekend of faith-sharing and during it she helped to lead a craft workshop for children and adults. It did some good work, although the children were quite disruptive. Later, in a team meeting, Linda told us of her disappointment that the disruption meant she had not had the in-depth discussions she had hoped for.

What do we do with that kind of experience? A lot will depend on our basic attitudes.

That is when this passage from Philippians 2 may help us. Its well-known exhortation to unity and our attitudes to one another can speak to our attitude in evangelism.

It falls into two obvious sections.

UNITY IN LOVE

The primary concern of Paul in writing is our unity as Christians in Christ, and that is a fundamental foundation for evangelism. As the old saying had it in pre-ironic days, 'See how these Christians love one another.'

If you have received any encouragement, love, fellowship, compassion, if you've received any of these wonderful qualities in your Christian life—and the chances are that you have—then this is how to see them: they call you to unity of love and purpose (v. 1–2).

With two colleagues, I took part in a classroom discussion with Year Six children. For an hour we had the opportunity to respond to some very searching and serious questions, as eleven-year-olds can ask: 'Do you believe what it says in the Bible?' 'What happens when you die?' 'Do you think that dinosaurs really existed?'

We gave our answers in unity, but not unison, because we had established enough fellowship and respect and love between us.

So here is a primary quality for evangelism: unity in love.

THE EXAMPLE OF JESUS

Here we move to the second and longer section of our passage (vv. 5–11): The call to unity in love is grounded securely in the example of Jesus. It is not simply a good idea, but the pattern of Jesus' life, the attitude with which he lived.

That attitude is fundamentally one of self-emptying, leading to God exalting him. The theological word for the self-emptying is *kenosis*, and we might therefore describe the attitude we should have as kenotic evangelism, or more simply as 'giving it away'.

For Jesus descends and is raised. He gives up his position of equality with the Father, plumbs the depths and is raised to the Father's right hand.

The pattern of his life is U-shaped:

135

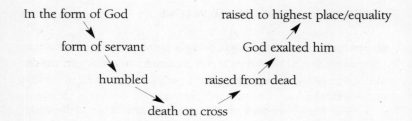

In the form of God

form of servant

humbled

death on cross

raised to highest place/equality

God exalted him

raised from dead

Here is the pattern of Jesus' life. Here is the pattern for our lives. Here is the pattern for our evangelism.

The pattern is not to hold tight to what God has given us—beauty, intelligence, the gift of the gab, love, compassion—but to let go of them in order that God may use us, and in his time raise us up.

This isn't easy: Richard was president of a university Christian Union and left when I did in the 1970s. He went to India with a mission group. He was a very gifted and intelligent man, who gave up status, career and money to do this. After six months in India, he was drowned in a river. Many people felt it was a shocking waste of a life.

Someone I knew slightly had left university at the same time, and moved to the same town as me. She sought me out to ask for advice and help. To my shame, I made some crass comments about Richard wanting to do God's will, and going to be with the Lord. In a sense this was true, but it was not done sensitively, as I realized rather quickly. Understandably, my acquaintance went elsewhere for the help she needed and deserved.

However, for all their insensitivity, I believe that behind my words there was something true about our lives as Christians and about our evangelism: it *is* about giving up status, prospects and power in order to be used by God.

This idea of 'giving it up' is not a random thought from one passage of the New Testament: the hymn from Philippians 2 is rightly seen as an important statement about Christ, and we can find many hymns, ancient and modern, that draw on it, such as

'And can it be', 'Meekness and majesty' or 'I will offer up my life'.

Paul uses a similar kenotic image in 2 Corinthians 8:9: 'Though he was rich, yet for your sakes he became poor, so that... you might become rich'. We see the same attitude in Jesus' own words: 'Whoever wishes to become great... must be slave of all' (Mark 10:43–44). We see it in Jesus' actions: taking the towel of the slave, he washed the feet of his disciples (John 13:3–17).

Our attitude in evangelism is to be modelled on that of Jesus, to be kenotic, to let go, trusting that God will raise us up.

In practical terms, it is well demonstrated by the 'servant evangelism' developed by some churches, for example cleaning up streets, washing cars for free, providing a present-wrapping service at a Christmas market, offering to pray for people.

Such practices especially highlight the servant nature of evangelism, but all evangelism, whatever the methods, is to be servant or kenotic evangelism at heart. Then it will be living out our unity in love, after the pattern and example of Jesus himself.

QUESTIONS FOR REFLECTION AND DISCUSSION

1. What do you find most helpful and most challenging in the attitude of Jesus?
2. Think of a time when you were able to share something of your faith: what was your attitude towards other people?
3. What practical steps can you take, with others, to demonstrate 'servant evangelism'?

SUGGESTIONS FOR FURTHER GROWTH

1. Be involved in sharing your faith through your local church, house group, work-based fellowship or whatever is appropriate. There is nothing like practice for growing!
2. Keep reading your Bible, asking yourself what you may learn about the motives for evangelism and the practice of evangelism.
3. Consider how you might use some of the excellent resources around, such as Alpha, Emmaus or Lost for Words. Besides the basic evangelistic course, these resources are developing into ranges of material, including Bible studies, aimed at supporting the growth of Christians, both new and mature.

NOTES

1   Published by Polity Press, 2000.
2   Published by Abingdon Press, 1993.
3   See Michael V. Fox, *A Time to Tear Down and a Time to Build Up: A Rereading of Ecclesiastes*, Eerdmans, 1999, pp. 27–49.
4   Fox, pp. 140–45.
5   'The Hound of Heaven' is a poem by the 19th-century poet Francis Thompson, in which he sees God in the form of a large hound pursuing him. At first, he flees in panic, but eventually realizes that God wishes him well and will not let him get away.
6   Based on a sermon preached at St Nicholas Church, Durham, on 18 August 2002.
7   W. Barclay: *The Gospel of Luke*, 9th impression, St Andrew's Press, 1965, p. 83.
8   I.H. Marshall: *The Gospel of Luke*, Paternoster, 1978, p. 304.
9   See the article 'Prostitute' in J.B. Green, S. McKnight, I.H. Marshall (eds.): *Dictionary of Jesus and the Gospels*, IVP, 1992, p. 643.
10 Barclay, p. 94.
11 H. Oppenheimer, 'Spirit and Body', *Theology* 93 (1990), pp. 133–141.
12 H. Oppenheimer, *Finding and Following: Talking with Children about God*, SCM, 1994.

LOST FOR WORDS

For all who think evangelism is not for them

JAMES LAWRENCE

Evangelism—the dreaded E word. Do you go hot and cold at the thought of talking to others about your Christian faith? This book grapples with how we can speak about our faith in a relaxed, natural and helpful way.

Based on the highly successful *Lost for Words* course run by CPAS, the book shows how in fact we don't have to be evangelists to be involved in God's ongoing work of evangelism. Rather, we can simply relax into 'being ourselves, with God, for others'.

ISBN 1 84101 096 0   £6.99

Available from your local Christian bookshop or direct from BRF using the order form on page 143.

LISTENING TO PEOPLE OF OTHER FAITHS

CLAIRE DISBREY

The world has changed. Once it seemed easy to say that only Christians knew the truth about God, and that they should go and share this truth with the 'lost'. These days, many of us live and work with people who are deeply committed to other faiths. Respect for people's beliefs is essential to life in a diverse society, but does that mean we have to embrace the idea that all religions are basically saying the same thing or leading us by different routes to the same God? How do Christians reconcile this situation with their longing —and Jesus' command—to share our faith?

Here is an opportunity to listen to ordinary people, who follow other faiths, talking about their experience of God, prayer, worship and ethical living. It offers the chance to hear before we speak, and to avoid making assumptions about how other faiths work in people's lives. Author Claire Disbrey reflects on these conversations to try to find ways forward for sensitive sharing of the Christian worldview today.

ISBN 1 84101 184 3   £7.99

Available from your local Christian bookshop or direct from BRF using the order form on page 143.

brf

Resourcing your spiritual journey

through...

- Bible reading notes
- Books for Advent & Lent
- Books for Bible study and prayer
- Books to resource those working with under 11s in school, church and at home

- Quiet days and retreats
- Training for primary teachers and children's leaders
- Godly Play
- Barnabas Live

For more information, visit the **brf** website at **www.brf.org.uk**